MW01044689

Gooseberry Patch

Church Suppers

Best-loved recipes from church gatherings and community get-togethers!

Gooseberry Patch

An imprint of Globe Pequot
246 Goose Lane
Guilford, CT 06437

www.gooseberrypatch.com

1·800·854·6673

Copyright 2019, Gooseberry Patch 978-1-62093-355-8

All rights reserved. No part of this book may be reproduced or utilized in any form or by any means, electronic or mechanical, including photocopying and recording, or by any information storage and retrieval system, without permission in writing from the publisher. Printed in Korea.

Do you have a tried & true recipe...

tip, craft or memory that you'd like to see featured in a **Gooseberry Patch** cookbook? Visit our website at **www.gooseberrypatch.com**, register and follow the easy steps to submit your favorite family recipe. Or send them to us at:

Gooseberry Patch
PO Box 812
Columbus, OH 43216-0812

Don't forget to include the number of servings your recipe makes, plus your name, address, phone number and email address. If we select your recipe, your name will appear right along with it... and you'll receive a **FREE** copy of the book!

Contents

Dedication

To everyone who loves a good old-fashioned church supper or ice cream social.

Appreciation

Sincere thanks to all the wonderful cooks who shared their crowd-pleasing, time-tested recipes with us!

Pancake Breakfasts

Triple-Berry Pancakes

6-1/2 oz. pkg.
  triple-berry muffin
  mix
1 T. all-purpose flour
2/3 c. water

2 T. oil
1 egg, beaten
Garnish: powdered
  sugar or pancake
  syrup

Stir together first 5 ingredients. Drop by
1/4 cupfuls onto a lightly greased griddle
or skillet over medium heat. Cook for about
3 minutes, until golden; flip pancakes
and cook for an additional 3 minutes on
the other side. Serve warm, sprinkled
with powdered sugar or with syrup on
the side. Makes about 8 pancakes.

Light & Fluffy Pancakes

Barbara Janssen
Beach Park, IL

*Topped with jam, jelly, preserves or syrup...
these just can't be beat.*

1 c. all-purpose flour
2 T. sugar
2 t. baking powder
1/2 t. salt

1 egg, beaten
1 c. milk
2 T. oil

Stir together flour, sugar, baking powder and salt. Add egg, milk and oil all at once to flour mixture, stirring until blended but still slightly lumpy. Pour batter onto a hot, lightly greased griddle or heavy skillet, about 1/4 cup each for regular pancakes or one tablespoon for silver dollar pancakes. Cook on both sides until golden, turning when surface is bubbly and edges are slightly dry. Makes about 8, 4-inch pancakes or about 30 silver dollar pancakes.

When you're making pancakes for a crowd, keep them warm in a low-temperature oven. Just arrange pancakes on a baking sheet, set in the oven, then serve as needed.

Triple-Berry Pancakes

Jennie Gist
Gooseberry Patch

*A griddle is hot enough for pancakes when a
few drops of water sprinkled on it dance around.*

6-1/2 oz. pkg. triple-berry
   muffin mix
1 T. all-purpose flour
2/3 c. water

2 T. oil
1 egg, beaten
Garnish: powdered sugar
   or maple syrup

Stir together muffin mix, flour, water, oil and egg. Drop by 1/4 cupfuls
onto a lightly greased griddle or skillet over medium heat. Cook
for about 3 minutes, until golden; flip pancakes and cook for an
additional 3 minutes on other side. Serve warm, sprinkled with
powdered sugar or with syrup on the side. Makes about
8, 4-inch pancakes.

Rise & shine centerpieces in seconds! Set a votive in
each of the cups of mini muffin tins, or tuck a cheery
bouquet in a vintage pitcher or teapot.

Southern-Style Breakfast Casserole

*Joyce Boswell
Lewisport, KY*

*If I didn't bring this to breakfast on Palm Sunday...
I don't think they'd let me in the door!*

2 lbs. ground pork sausage,
   browned and drained
4 eggs, beaten
1/2 c. milk
1 onion, diced
6 c. crispy rice cereal

2 c. cooked rice
10-3/4 oz. can cream of
   chicken soup
10-3/4 oz. cream of celery soup
8-oz. pkg. shredded Cheddar
   cheese

Combine all ingredients in a large bowl. Pour into a lightly greased 13"x9" baking pan. Bake, uncovered, at 425 degrees for 45 minutes. Serves 8 to 10.

Sweet Ham

*Kerry Mayer
Dunham Springs, LA*

*A slow-cooker favorite...so easy to prepare
and always delicious.*

7-lb. fully-cooked ham
2 c. orange juice
1/2 c. water

20-oz. can crushed pineapple
3 T. brown sugar, packed

Place ham in a slow cooker. Pour orange juice, water and pineapple over top; sprinkle with brown sugar. Cover and cook on low setting for 8 hours. Serves 24.

Friends and acquaintances add much to the richness of life...
—James E. Faust

Golden French Toast

Brenda Rieter
Middlefield, OH

Baked in the oven, this breakfast treat is a snap to make.
Top servings with a dusting of powdered sugar.

1 loaf bread, cubed and divided
8-oz. pkg. cream cheese,
    softened and cubed
10 eggs, beaten

1-1/2 c. half-and-half
1/2 c. butter, melted
1/4 c. maple syrup

Layer half the bread in a greased 13"x9" baking pan; top with cream cheese. Place remaining bread over the top; set aside. Beat eggs, half-and-half, butter and syrup together; pour over bread. Refrigerate overnight; bake at 350 degrees for 40 to 50 minutes. Serves 8 to 10.

Everyone loves the taste of fresh-squeezed juice.
Set a big bowl of orange and grapefruit halves
on a serving table, along with some juicers.

Grandma Kansas' Cinnamon Rolls

Diana Pike
Mount Vernon, OH

This recipe was given to my husband by his grandmother who lived in Kansas. She made these every time the family got together. Family and church members have enjoyed these rich gooey treats for 4 generations!

2 loaves frozen bread dough, thawed
1 c. butter, softened and divided
1-1/2 c. sugar, divided
1/4 c. cinnamon, divided
1-1/2 c. brown sugar, packed and divided
2 12-oz. cans evaporated milk

Place each dough loaf in a large greased bowl; let rise until double in bulk. Punch each down. Roll out each loaf into a 12"x20" rectangle on a well floured surface. Spread half the butter on each rectangle; sprinkle each with half the sugar. Sprinkle half each of the cinnamon and brown sugar over sugar. Roll up each rectangle jelly-roll style, starting at the long end. Slice each roll into 12 slices. Arrange rolls in 2 greased 13"x9" baking pans. Cover with plastic wrap; let rise in a warm place for 45 minutes, until double in bulk. Pour one can evaporated milk over each pan of rolls. Bake at 400 degrees for 25 to 30 minutes, until golden; ingredients may bubble over pan sides as rolls are baking. Remove from oven; let stand for 5 minutes. Invert each pan onto a baking sheet; serve warm. Makes 2 dozen.

Offer a variety of syrups, butter, honey butter, jams and jellies on a small table that's separate from the breakfast serving table. Everyone can choose their favorite toppings while the buffet line keeps moving.

Cherry Coffee Cake

Flo Burtnett
Gage, OK

*Sweet and fruity, this coffee cake is a scrumptious
addition to any breakfast table.*

1 egg, beaten
milk
1/2 c. margarine, softened
1 c. sugar

2 c. all-purpose flour
2 t. baking powder
2 21-oz. cans cherry pie filling

Break egg into a measuring cup; add enough milk to measure one cup
and set aside. Combine margarine, sugar, flour and baking powder.
Add egg mixture; mix well. Pour batter into a greased 13"x9" baking
pan. Spread pie filling evenly over top; sprinkle with topping. Bake at
350 degrees for 40 minutes. Serves 10 to 12.

Topping:

1 c. all-purpose flour
1 c. sugar

1/2 c. margarine, softened

Combine all ingredients until crumbly.

Serving up toast? Pull out your cookie cutters and cut toast
into whimsical shapes. Mini cookie cutters are just the right
size for making the sweetest pats of butter too!

Feather-Light Waffles

Suzanne Williams
Azusa, CA

*I've found for the best results, if your home is warmer than
70 degrees, the yeast mixture should be refrigerated overnight.*

1/2 c. water
1 env. active dry yeast
2 c. milk
1/2 c. butter, melted
1 t. sugar

1 t. salt
2 c. all-purpose flour
2 eggs, beaten
1/4 t. baking soda

Heat water to 115 degrees; sprinkle yeast over water. Let stand
5 minutes. Heat milk to 115 degrees; add to yeast mixture along with
butter, sugar, salt and flour. Beat until smooth. Cover bowl with plastic
wrap; let stand overnight. Beat eggs and baking soda into batter
(batter will be thin). Spoon between 1/2 and 3/4 cup batter onto a
lightly greased waffle iron. Bake following manufacturer's directions.
Makes 8 waffles.

Dress up paper napkins in no time at all,
simply trim the edged with decorative-edged scissors!

Pancake Breakfasts

Old-Fashioned Blueberry Pancakes

Sharon Sorrels
Troutville, VA

*An all-time favorite...try topping pancakes
with blueberry syrup for a very, berry flavor!*

1 c. milk
1 egg
1/4 c. sour cream
1 c. all-purpose flour
1 T. baking powder

1 T. sugar
1/4 t. salt
2 T. oil
1/2 c. blueberries

Combine milk, egg and sour cream; beat well. Stir together flour,
baking powder, sugar and salt; add to milk mixture. Beat until lumps
disappear; mix in oil. Fold in blueberries; pour 1/4 cup batter per
pancake onto a greased hot griddle. Flip when bubbles appear. Makes
one dozen.

Kids will giggle when you serve up silly pancake animals!
Simply put batter into a plastic zipping bag, snip off a
corner and squeeze batter into a greased, hot skillet
or griddle in fun shapes.

Make-Ahead Ham & Cheese Casserole

Wendy Deckman
Corona, CA

This is one of our favorites for early morning Bible study or mothers' group get-togethers. Remember to prepare this recipe in advance...you'll need to refrigerate it 24 hours before baking.

1 loaf sliced bread, divided and
    crusts trimmed
10 to 12 slices deli ham,
    chopped
6-oz. jar sliced mushrooms,
    drained
10 to 12 slices Cheddar cheese

6 eggs
3 c. milk
1/2 t. dry mustard
2 c. corn flake cereal, crushed
1/2 c. butter, melted

Arrange to fit about 8 bread slices in a greased 13"x9" baking pan. Add sliced ham; sprinkle with mushrooms. Arrange cheese slices over mushrooms. Top with remaining bread. Beat together eggs, milk and mustard; pour over bread. Refrigerate for 24 hours. Just before baking, combine cereal and butter; sprinkle over top. Bake, uncovered, at 350 degrees for one hour. Serves 10 to 12.

A roomy, ice-filled galvanized tub is perfect for keeping cartons of milk and juice frosty. You can even pick up pint-size cartons of milk...just right for little hands to hold.

Pancake Breakfasts

Rise & Shine Bacon Waffles

Tonya Sheppard
Galveston, TX

Bacon adds a terrific flavor to morning waffles...
you'll love 'em served alongside scrambled eggs.

1-3/4 c. all-purpose flour
1 T. sugar
2 t. baking powder
1/2 t. salt
3 eggs, separated

1-1/2 c. milk
1/4 c. butter, melted
1 lb. bacon, crisply cooked
   and crumbled

Combine flour, sugar, baking powder and salt in a large bowl; set aside. Beat together egg yolks, milk and butter; stir into dry ingredients until smooth. Beat egg whites in a mixing bowl until stiff peaks form; fold into batter. Stir in bacon. Pour between 1/2 and 3/4 cup onto in a lightly greased waffle iron; bake according to manufacturer's directions until golden. Makes 8 waffles.

While orange and grapefruit are oh-so refreshing,
don't forget about white grape, tomato, pineapple,
cranberry and apple juices too!

Make-Ahead Scrambled Eggs

Dana Thompson
Delaware, OH

Start this the night before...so easy and so delicious!

3 T. butter, divided
2 doz. eggs, beaten and divided
1/2 c. milk
10-3/4 oz. can cream of
   mushroom soup
4-oz. can sliced mushrooms,
   drained

1/2 c. green pepper, chopped
1/2 c. onion, chopped
1 c. pasteurized process cheese
   spread, cubed

Melt half the butter in a large skillet over medium heat. Add half the eggs; cook until lightly set. Place in a lightly greased 13"x9" baking pan. Melt remaining butter in skillet; scramble remaining eggs. Add to eggs already in baking pan. Combine milk and soup; pour over eggs. Top with mushrooms, pepper, onion and cheese. Refrigerate overnight. Bake, covered, at 300 degrees for one hour. Serves 10 to 12.

Kids will love this...serve their favorite flavor
of yogurt as a yummy dip for fresh fruit!

Pancake Breakfasts

Laura's Eggs Benedict

Laura Fuller
Fort Wayne, IN

You can easily substitute split biscuits for the English muffins and even a sausage patty for the Canadian bacon...tasty either way.

4 English muffins, split and
    toasted
16 slices Canadian bacon
8 eggs
1/4 c. plus 1 T. butter
1/4 c. all-purpose flour
1 t. paprika

1/8 t. nutmeg
2 c. milk
8-oz. pkg. shredded Swiss
    cheese
1/2 c. chicken broth
1 c. corn flake cereal, crushed

Arrange muffins split-side up in a lightly greased 13"x9" baking pan. Place 2 bacon slices on each muffin half. Fill a large skillet halfway with water; bring to just boiling. Break one egg into a dish; carefully slide into water. Repeat with 3 more eggs. Simmer, uncovered, for 3 minutes, or just until set. Remove eggs with a slotted spoon. Repeat with remaining eggs. Place one egg on each muffin; set aside. In a saucepan over medium heat, melt 1/4 cup butter; stir in flour, paprika and nutmeg. Add milk; cook and stir until thick and bubbly. Stir in cheese until melted; add broth. Carefully spoon sauce over eggs. Melt remaining butter; stir in cereal and sprinkle over top. Chill overnight. Bake, uncovered, at 375 degrees for 20 to 25 minutes, until heated through. Serves 8.

Milk bottles or Mason jars make perfect posy holders.
Tuck the bottles or jars inside an old-fashioned
milk bottle carrier...so sweet.

Apple & Spice Baked French Toast

Andrea Beck
Boise, ID

French toast with a twist...yum!

1 loaf French bread, sliced
8 eggs
3-1/2 c. milk
1 c. sugar, divided
1 T. vanilla extract
6 to 8 apples, cored, peeled and
    sliced

1 T. cinnamon
1 t. nutmeg
2 T. butter, diced
Garnish: warm maple syrup

Place bread in a greased 13"x9" baking pan; set aside. Beat eggs, milk, 1/2 cup sugar and vanilla together; pour half of mixture over bread. Layer apples over bread; pour remaining egg mixture over the top. Set aside. Combine remaining sugar, cinnamon and nutmeg; sprinkle over apples. Dot with butter; cover and refrigerate overnight. Bake at 350 degrees for one hour, until lightly golden. Remove from oven; let stand for 5 to 10 minutes before serving. Slice into squares and serve with warm maple syrup. Serves 8 to 10.

A table runner really dresses up a table, and you can make one in no time at all. Just tie together the corners of several vintage-style tea towels!

18

Pancake Breakfasts

Classic Oatmeal Waffles

Jamie Johnson
Hilliard, OH

*These are terrific served with Winter Morning Peaches
or any fruit-flavored syrup.*

2 eggs, beaten
2 c. buttermilk
1 c. quick-cooking oats,
　uncooked
1 T. molasses
1 T. oil

1 c. whole-wheat flour
1 t. baking soda
1 t. baking powder
1/2 t. salt
milk

Whisk together eggs and buttermilk in a large bowl. Add oats; mix well. Stir in molasses and oil. Combine flour, baking soda, baking powder and salt in a large bowl; stir into egg mixture. Thin with a little milk, if necessary. Pour about 3/4 cup batter onto a lightly greased waffle iron. Bake according to manufacturer's directions. Makes 5 waffles.

Winter Morning Peaches

Cheri Emery
Quincy, IL

A scrumptious way to enjoy peaches.

2　16-oz. cans sliced peaches
2 T. butter
1/3 c. brown sugar, packed

1/2 t. cinnamon
2 T. cornstarch
1/4 c. cold water

Heat peaches, butter, brown sugar and cinnamon in a saucepan over medium heat. Combine cornstarch and cold water; add to peaches and cook about 4 to 5 minutes, until thickened. Serve over pancakes or waffles. Makes about 4 cups.

Oven-Baked Pepper Bacon

John Alexander
New Britain, CT

The ground pepper adds a wonderful flavor to the bacon.

1-1/2 lbs. bacon slices   2-1/2 t. coarsely ground pepper

Arrange bacon slices in 2 ungreased 15"x10" jelly-roll pans. Sprinkle with pepper. Bake at 400 degrees for 25 minutes, switching pans between upper and lower racks halfway through. Remove bacon when crisply cooked. Drain on paper towels. Serves 12.

Arrange flatware in coffee or teapots
for a cheery breakfast welcome.

Kristen's Breakfast Bake

Kristen Nicholson
Norwood, MA

I first made this for my son Joseph's christening brunch where it was a huge hit. It's so easy to multiply for any size group, that now I get requests to bring it to every get-together.

2 12-oz. pkgs. ground pork
   sausage
1 green pepper, chopped
1 onion, chopped
3 c. frozen diced potatoes
1 c. biscuit baking mix

2 c. milk
4 eggs, beaten
8-oz. pkg. shredded Cheddar
   cheese, divided
1/4 t. pepper

Brown sausage in a large skillet over medium heat. Add green pepper and onion. Sauté just until vegetables are tender; drain. Transfer sausage mixture into a lightly greased 13"x9" baking pan. Add frozen potatoes; toss to mix. Combine biscuit mix, milk, eggs, 1-1/2 cups cheese and pepper in a large bowl; fold into sausage mixture, mixing well. Bake, uncovered, at 400 degrees for 40 minutes, until set. Sprinkle with remaining cheese; bake for an additional 5 to 8 minutes, until cheese is melted and bubbly. Serves 12.

Keep an eye open at tag sales for vintage tart tins, gelatin molds, bread or pie pans. They always have clever designs and are just right for filling with napkins, flatware, sugar packets or tea bags.

Chocolate Buttermilk Biscuits

Kathy Grashoff
Fort Wayne, IN

Top these biscuits with orange marmalade or raspberry jam…
perfect pairing with their chocolate flavor.

3 T. sugar, divided
1/8 t. cinnamon
2 c. all-purpose flour
1 T. baking powder
1/3 c. butter

3/4 c. buttermilk
1/2 c. semi-sweet chocolate
  chips
1/4 c. butter, melted

Combine 2 tablespoons sugar and cinnamon; set aside. Combine flour, remaining sugar and baking powder; cut in butter until mixture is crumbly. Add buttermilk and chocolate chips, stirring just until dry ingredients are moistened. Turn dough out onto a lightly floured surface; knead 3 to 4 times. Roll dough to 1/2-inch thickness; cut with 2-1/4 inch round cookie or biscuit cutter. Arrange biscuits on a lightly greased baking sheet; sprinkle with sugar mixture. Bake at 425 degrees for 15 minutes, or until golden. Brush with melted butter. Makes one dozen.

Check with your local orchard or at the farmers' market
and pick up some wooden fruit crates and bushel baskets…
they make easy work of toting breakfast fixin's from
the car to the church kitchen!

Monkey Bread

Michelle Pettit
Sebree, KY

This is really quick & easy and always a big hit.
I usually have to make two because our preacher
will try to sneak away with one to take home!

1/2 c. sugar	1 c. brown sugar, packed
1-1/2 t. cinnamon	1/2 c. butter, melted
3 12-oz. tubes refrigerated biscuits, quartered	2 T. water

Combine sugar and cinnamon in a bowl. Roll biscuit pieces in sugar mixture; place in a greased Bundt® pan. Combine brown sugar, butter and water; pour over biscuits. Bake at 350 degrees for 30 minutes. Invert onto serving plate. Serves 6 to 8.

When you spice a dish with love,
it'll tickle every palate.
–Titus Maccius Plautus

Savory Stuffed French Toast

Danielle Keeney
Kutztown, PA

Stuffed with cheese and sausage...sure to be a new favorite.

8 thick slices French bread
2 T. butter, softened
8-oz. pkg. brown & serve
    sausage patties, browned,
    drained and cut into
    bite-size pieces

1 c. shredded Swiss cheese
2 eggs
1/2 c. milk
1-1/2 t. sugar
1/4 t. cinnamon

Cut a pocket in the crust of each slice of bread; spread butter in each pocket. Set aside. Combine sausage and cheese; stuff into pockets. Beat together eggs, milk, sugar and cinnamon in a shallow bowl; dip bread in mixture. Cook on a greased griddle until both sides are golden. Serves 4.

Be sure to set out table tents so everyone
knows what's cookin' for breakfast!

Pancake Breakfasts

Banana-Nut Pancakes

Karen Norman
Jacksonville, FL

Kids will love these!

2 c. all-purpose flour
2 T. sugar
1 T. baking powder
1 t. baking soda
1/2 t. salt

2 eggs, beaten
1-3/4 c. buttermilk
2 T. oil
2 bananas, mashed
1/2 c. chopped pecans

Combine flour, sugar, baking powder, baking soda and salt; add eggs, buttermilk and oil. Stir until just mixed; mix in bananas and pecans. Pour 1/4 cup batter per pancake onto a greased skillet; cook over medium heat until golden on both sides. Makes 20 to 24 pancakes.

Toffee French Toast

Michelle Younkman
Lewisville, TX

Long lines form when you serve this up for breakfast.

6 T. butter
6 T. brown sugar, packed
6 T. corn syrup

1 c. milk
1 egg
6 slices bread

Combine butter, brown sugar and corn syrup in a saucepan; bring to a boil. Stir for 2 minutes. Pour into a lightly greased 13"x9" baking pan; set aside. Beat milk and egg together; dip each slice of bread in mixture. Place in baking pan; bake at 450 degrees for 6 to 8 minutes. Turn; bake for an additional 6 to 8 minutes. Makes 6 servings.

Toss a little fun into your pancakes...chocolate chips, berries and chopped nuts all are tasty surprises.

Caramel Breakfast Ring

JoAnne Murdock
Hilliard, OH

This is wonderful for those family & friends gatherings!

1 c. chopped pecans, divided
16 frozen dinner rolls
3-1/2 oz. pkg. cook & serve
    butterscotch pudding mix

3/4 c. brown sugar, packed
1/2 c. butter, melted

Sprinkle a lightly greased Bundt® pan with half the pecans. Arrange dinner rolls over pecans; sprinkle with pudding mix. Combine brown sugar and butter; pour over rolls. Sprinkle with remaining pecans. Let stand overnight at room temperature. Bake, uncovered, at 325 degrees for 30 minutes. Invert onto a serving platter. Serves 8 to 12.

If you're baking a breakfast casserole or quiche at home first, keep it piping hot by wrapping the baking pan in a layer of aluminum foil, then top with layers of newspaper.

Crustless Bacon-Swiss Quiche

Sharon Monroe
Concord, NH

With one less step, this quiche recipe is a real time saver.

9 eggs, beaten
3 c. milk
1 t. dry mustard
salt and pepper to taste
9 slices white bread, crusts
    trimmed

1-1/2 c. Swiss cheese, diced
1-lb. pkg. bacon, crisply cooked
    and crumbled

Combine eggs, milk, mustard, salt and pepper; blend well. Tear bread into small pieces; add to egg mixture along with cheese and bacon. Pour into a greased 13"x9" baking pan or 2 greased 9" glass pie plates. Refrigerate for 2 hours to overnight. Bake at 350 degrees until eggs have set, 45 to 50 minutes. Cut into squares or wedges. Serves 12.

No need to slice and serve...bake a quiche in muffin or custard cups for oh-so simple individual servings. When making minis, reduce the baking time by about 10 minutes, and slide a toothpick into each to check for doneness.

Homestyle Sausage Gravy & Biscuits

Amy Butcher
Columbus, GA

This is a southern favorite for breakfast.

3 c. milk
6 T. all-purpose flour

salt and pepper to taste
1/2 lb. ground pork sausage

Whisk together milk, flour, salt and pepper in a large bowl until smooth. Pour into a large skillet; simmer over medium heat, stirring constantly for 15 minutes. Brown sausage in a separate skillet over medium heat; drain. Stir sausage into gravy. Ladle sausage gravy over split biscuits. Serves 10.

Biscuits:

2-3/4 c. biscuit baking mix

3/4 c. milk

Combine biscuit mix and milk until soft dough forms. Drop by spoonfuls onto ungreased baking sheets. Bake at 450 degrees for 10 minutes, or until golden. Makes 8 to 10.

Slide melon balls, strawberries, pineapple chunks and banana slices onto small wooden skewers...what an easy way to serve fruit!

Tex-Mex Sausage Casserole

Vickie
Gooseberry Patch

*A slow-cooker casserole that's ideal for a breakfast with family &
friends. For a real kick, add some chopped jalapeños to taste!*

1-lb. pkg. ground breakfast
   sausage, browned and
   drained
4-oz. can diced green chiles
1 onion, diced

1 green pepper, diced
2-1/2 c. shredded Monterey Jack
   or Pepper Jack cheese
18 eggs, beaten
Garnish: sour cream, salsa

In a greased slow cooker, layer half each sausage, chiles, onion,
pepper and cheese. Repeat layering with remaining ingredients except
eggs and garnish, ending with cheese. Pour beaten eggs over top.
Cover and cook on low setting for 7 to 8 hours. Serve with sour
cream and salsa. Serves 12.

How about setting up a cereal station for breakfast?
Pitchers of icy-cold milk paired with a variety of
cereals and fruit are tasty. You can even have
packets of instant oatmeal on hand.

Buttermilk Pancakes

Rita Morgan
Pueblo, CO

*Fluffy and golden, these pancakes are just like
the ones from Grandma's kitchen.*

1-3/4 c. all-purpose flour	2 eggs
2 T. sugar	2 c. buttermilk
2 t. baking powder	1/4 c. oil
1 t. baking soda	1/2 t. vanilla extract
1/2 t. salt	

Combine first 5 ingredients in a large bowl; set aside. Beat together eggs, buttermilk, oil and vanilla in a mixing bowl; stir into flour mixture just until moistened. Pour batter by 1/4 cupfuls onto a greased hot griddle. Turn when bubbles appear on surface; cook until golden. Serves 6.

Fruity Pancake Topping

Tori Willis
Champaign, IL

*Try this fruity sauce spooned over pancakes,
waffles or French toast.*

1/2 c. brown sugar, packed	2 bananas, sliced
10-oz. pkg. frozen raspberries, thawed	8-oz. can pineapple chunks, drained

Combine all ingredients in a blender; process until blended. Transfer to a saucepan; simmer over low heat until heated through. Makes about 3 cups.

I am beginning to learn that it is the sweet and simple things
of life which are the real ones after all.

– Laura Ingalls Wilder

Ladies' Lunch

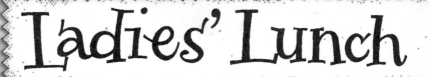

Heavenly Chicken Salad

8 c. cooked chicken,
   chopped
2 c. seedless grapes,
   quartered

2 c. celery, chopped
1 c. chopped pecans
1 c. mayonnaise
3/4 t. pepper

Combine all ingredients; refrigerate until
ready to serve. Serves 18 as a salad,
20 to 30 as a sandwich on croissants.

Golden Chicken Divan

Amy Kim
Ann Arbor, MI

*Always a favorite at church potlucks...quick & easy
to make and bakes in just 15 minutes.*

1 lb. broccoli, chopped
1-1/2 c. cooked chicken, cubed
10-3/4 oz. can cream of broccoli
   soup
1/3 c. sour cream
1/2 t. garlic powder

1/2 t. onion powder
1/4 t. seasoned salt
1/2 c. shredded Cheddar cheese
1 T. butter, melted
2 T. bread crumbs

Cover broccoli with water in a saucepan; bring to a boil over medium heat. Cook for 5 minutes, or until tender; drain. In a large bowl, combine broccoli, chicken, soup, sour cream, garlic powder, onion powder and salt. Spread in a greased 8"x8" baking pan; sprinkle with cheese. Mix together melted butter and bread crumbs; sprinkle over cheese. Bake, uncovered, at 450 degrees for 15 minutes, or until bubbly and golden. Serves 6.

When setting up for a luncheon, it's so easy to tote napkins and silverware from table to table...simply tuck them into a vintage milk bottle carrier.

Bishop's Chicken

Doris Zinck
Lincoln University, PA

This is a recipe that was prepared for a luncheon following church services the Bishop presided over. Note that you'll want to start this one day in advance.

2 3-lb. chickens
1 c. white wine or chicken broth
1 c. water
1-1/2 t. salt
1/2 t. curry powder
1 onion, sliced
1/2 c. celery, sliced

2 6-oz. pkgs. long grain &
  wild rice, uncooked
2 8-oz. pkgs. sliced mushrooms
1/4 c. butter
8-oz. container sour cream
10-3/4 oz. can golden
  mushroom soup

Combine chickens and next 6 ingredients in a large soup pot. Bring to a boil over medium-high heat; reduce heat and simmer for one hour. Cool. Remove and discard bones and skin. Reserve broth and chicken; refrigerate overnight. Next day, skim fat from surface of broth. In a large saucepan, combine rice and reserved broth, adding enough water to cook according to package directions. Stir in chicken and set aside. In a skillet, sauté mushrooms in butter; add to chicken mixture. Combine sour cream and soup; stir into chicken mixture. Spoon into a greased 13"x9" baking pan. Bake, uncovered, at 350 degrees for one hour. Serves 8 to 10.

Sweet teapots make the prettiest posy holders...
centerpieces in a snap!

Kay's Chinese Chicken Salad

Linda Galvin
Ames, IA

Last year I hosted a ladies' potluck luncheon and my good friend Kay brought this salad. Everyone thought it was marvelous!

3-oz. pkg. chicken-flavored
 ramen noodles, uncooked
1 head cabbage, shredded
4 boneless, skinless chicken
 breasts, cooked and
 shredded

2 T. onion, chopped
2 T. slivered almonds, toasted
2 T. sesame seed, toasted

Set aside ramen noodle seasoning packet for dressing; crush noodles. Combine all ingredients except seasoning packet in a large serving bowl; toss lightly to combine. Drizzle with dressing and toss again. Serves 8 to 10.

Dressing:

1 c. oil
3 T. sugar
1/3 c. vinegar
1 t. pepper

2 t. salt
reserved ramen noodle
 seasoning packet

Whisk together all ingredients.

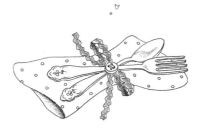

If you're preparing sandwiches before a get-together, wrap them up in wax paper. Tied with a length of rick rack or sealed with a sticker, they'll stay fresh and look oh-so-pretty.

Ladies' Lunch

Heavenly Chicken Salad

Patricia King
Portsmouth, VA

My girlfriend Glinda and I made this for our church bazaar luncheon. We've served this as a salad and as a sandwich on a croissant. Now it's been requested for 4 years in a row!

8 c. cooked chicken, chopped
2 c. seedless grapes, quartered
2 c. celery, chopped
1 c. chopped pecans
1 c. mayonnaise
1-1/2 t. salt
3/4 t. pepper

Combine all ingredients; refrigerate until ready to serve. Serves 18 as a salad, 20 to 30 as a sandwich on croissants.

Almond Tea Sandwiches

Michelle Sheridan
Delaware, OH

Serve these triangle-shaped sandwiches stacked on a tiered stand.

3/4 c. butter
2 t. lemon juice
1/8 t. salt
1/2 c. fresh basil, chopped
20 slices favorite bread
1 c. cooked chicken, finely chopped
1/2 c. mayonnaise
1/2 c. slivered almonds
salt and pepper to taste

Combine first 4 ingredients. Spread each slice of bread with a thin layer of butter mixture. Combine remaining ingredients; spread onto half the bread slices. Top with remaining bread slices butter-side down. Remove crusts; slice into triangles. Makes 40.

For a fruity, slightly sweet spin on savory chicken salads, dress them up with a sprinkle of sweetened, dried cranberries, mandarin oranges, pineapple or raisins.

Pasta Salad & Poppy Seed Dressing

Debbie Gasser
Castle Rock, CO

Filled with your favorite veggies,
this pasta salad is a winner.

16-oz. pkg. bowtie pasta, cooked
1 c. shredded Cheddar cheese
2 c. broccoli flowerets
1 c. carrots, peeled and sliced
1 c. cucumber, diced
1 c. cherry tomatoes, halved
1/2 c. green onion, chopped

Combine all ingredients in a large bowl; toss with Poppy Seed Dressing. Cover and refrigerate for at least one hour. Serves 16 to 18.

Poppy Seed Dressing:

1/2 c. cider vinegar
1/2 c. sugar
1 clove garlic, minced
1 green onion, chopped
1/2 t. dry mustard
1/2 t. salt
1 c. oil
1 T. poppy seed

In a blender, combine all ingredients except oil and poppy seed; process until well blended. Gradually add oil; blend until smooth. Stir in poppy seed.

Napkin rings are simple to make. Just sew buttons, charms or fabric yo-yo's onto a 6-inch length of elastic. Stitch the ends together and you're done!

Mom's Veggie Pizza

Beckie Kreml
Peebles, OH

My mom used to make this for church dinners and showers.
Now I make it for our fellowship Sunday after evening service.
It's easy to make and there are never leftovers!

2 8-oz. tubes refrigerated
   crescent rolls
8-oz. pkg. cream cheese,
   softened
1-oz. pkg. ranch salad
   dressing mix

4 c. favorite vegetables, finely
   chopped, such as broccoli,
   carrots, lettuce, tomatoes,
   peppers and onions
8-oz. pkg. shredded Cheddar
   cheese

Unroll crescent rolls and press onto an ungreased 15"x10" jelly-roll
pan. Bake according to package directions; cool. Combine cream
cheese and ranch dressing mix; spread over crust. Top with vegetables
and sprinkle with cheese; refrigerate until ready to serve. Makes about
16 servings.

Veggie Pizza variations are as easy as choosing your favorite
veggies, flavored cream cheese and shredded cheese. Try cutting
your pizza into bite-size squares for easy nibbling.

South-of-the-Border Chicken Soup

Paula Lee
Lapel, IN

*The ladies at church like this recipe because
it's healthy and best of all...easy!*

2 to 3 boneless, skinless
  chicken breasts
15-oz. can black beans, drained
  and rinsed
15-1/4 oz. can corn, drained

24-oz. jar salsa
tortilla chips
Garnish: sour cream, shredded
  Cheddar cheese

Layer chicken, beans, corn and salsa in a slow cooker. Cover and cook on low setting for 6 to 8 hours, until chicken is done. Using 2 forks, shred chicken and return to slow cooker; ladle into bowls. Serve with chips and garnish with desired toppings. Serves 6 to 8.

Add a bit of vintage charm to lunch...serve salads
and soups in dainty teacups.

Southwestern Layered Salad

Lori Downing
Bradenton, FL

*Not only does my family love this recipe, but when
I brought it to church I had many requests for it.*

15-oz. can black beans, drained
    and rinsed
1/4 c. salsa
2 c. lettuce, chopped
2 tomatoes, chopped
15-1/4 oz. can corn, drained

1 green pepper, chopped
1 red onion, finely chopped
1/2 c. shredded Cheddar cheese
1/4 c. bacon bits
Italian salad dressing to taste

Combine black beans and salsa in a small bowl. In a trifle bowl,
layer bean mixture, lettuce, tomatoes, corn, green pepper, onion and
cheese. Sprinkle with bacon bits; drizzle with dressing. Refrigerate
until ready to serve. Serves 8.

A new terra-cotta pot makes a terrific ice bucket if your ladies'
luncheon is outdoors. Simply line the pot with wax paper,
fill with ice and add a new garden trowel.

Spinach & Bacon Quiche

Jo Ann
Gooseberry Patch

*This classic combination is always popular
with a side of grapes or sliced melon.*

4 slices bacon, crisply cooked,
    crumbled and drippings
    reserved
1/2 c. onion, thinly sliced
2 c. baby spinach
9-inch pie crust, unbaked

1/2 c. fontina cheese, grated
5 eggs, beaten
1/4 c. whipping cream
1/2 c. milk
salt and pepper to taste
1/8 t. nutmeg

Heat reserved drippings in a large skillet over medium heat. Add
onion; cook until tender, about 3 minutes. Add spinach, one cup
at a time; cook just until wilted, about one minute. Cool. Sprinkle
bottom of pie crust with cheese. Evenly distribute bacon and spinach
mixture over cheese. Whisk together eggs, whipping cream and milk;
sprinkle with salt, pepper and nutmeg. Pour into pie crust. Bake at
375 degrees for 25 to 35 minutes; cool 5 to 10 minutes before
serving. Serves 6 to 8.

Make 'em mini...bake quiche ingredients in
mini Bundt® pans...oh-so pretty!

Garden-Fresh Zucchini Quiche

Lori Ritchey
Denver, PA

I love to bring this to church socials and family picnics
at the end of summer when zucchini is plentiful.

4 c. zucchini, grated
1-1/2 c. biscuit baking mix
1/2 c. oil
3 eggs, beaten
1 t. dried oregano

1/2 t. salt
1/2 t. pepper
1-1/2 c. shredded Cheddar
   cheese
1/2 c. onion, chopped

Mix together zucchini, baking mix, oil and eggs until well blended. Add remaining ingredients. Pour into a lightly greased 9" deep-dish pie plate. Bake at 400 degrees for 25 minutes. Serves 8.

Put a tiered pie stand to work serving mini quiches or muffins, fruit, cookies or candy. It's even great for holding napkins and flatware...perfect!

Creamy Chicken Lasagna

Kristi Root
Millersburg, OH

This is a simple and special lasagna with a wonderful flavor that everyone loves.

2 to 3 c. cooked chicken, diced
10-3/4 oz. can cream of chicken soup
10-3/4 oz. cream of mushroom soup
1/2 c. grated Parmesan cheese
8-oz. pkg. shredded mozzarella cheese, divided

8-oz. container sour cream
1 c. onion, finely chopped
1 c. sliced mushrooms
Optional: 1/4 c. chopped pimento
1/2 t. garlic powder
6 to 9 lasagna noodles, cooked

Combine chicken, soups, Parmesan cheese, 1/2 cup mozzarella cheese and remaining ingredients except lasagna noodles. In a lightly greased 13"x9" baking pan, layer chicken mixture and lasagna noodles. Repeat layering; sprinkle with remaining mozzarella. Bake, uncovered, at 350 degrees for 40 to 45 minutes. Let stand for 5 to 10 minutes before serving. Serves 6 to 8.

Vintage hankies are perfect for tying up little sachets.
Fill them with dried lavender, gather with a pretty ribbon and share with friends.

Pasta Bake Florentine

Jenny Flake
Gilbert, AZ

*This dish is a huge hit at our church dinner events
and is always the first to go. Not only is it
delicious, but so colorful and appealing.*

2 T. olive oil
1 onion, finely chopped
1/4 c. red pepper, chopped
1/2 c. mushrooms, coarsely
   chopped
1 lb. ground beef
1/2 t. salt
1/4 t. garlic salt
1/4 t. pepper

2 26-oz. jars pasta sauce
1 c. marinated artichokes,
   drained and chopped
10-oz. pkg. frozen spinach,
   thawed and drained
16-oz. pkg. rotini pasta, cooked
8-oz. pkg. shredded mozzarella
   cheese

Heat olive oil in a Dutch oven over medium heat. Sauté onion, red
pepper and mushrooms until tender, about 5 minutes. Stir in
ground beef, salt, garlic salt and pepper. Cook until beef is browned,
about 5 to 7 minutes; drain. Stir in pasta sauce, artichokes and
spinach until well combined. Stir in cooked pasta. Transfer to a lightly
greased 13"x9" baking pan; sprinkle with cheese. Bake, uncovered, at
350 degrees for 15 to 20 minutes, until heated through and cheese is
melted. Serves 8.

Turn pressed-glass jelly jars or pint-size Mason jars
into charming votive holders. Add coarse salt or
sea glass to each and nestle a votive inside.

Best-Ever Tortellini Salad

Priscilla Reed
Rindge, NH

This is an excellent salad for church socials.

2 9-oz. pkgs. cheese tortellini,
   cooked
2 red or green peppers, chopped
1 red onion, chopped
3.8-oz. can sliced black olives,
   drained
1/2 c. white vinegar
1/2 c. olive oil

3 T. fresh mint, chopped
3 T. lemon juice
2 T. cooking sherry or
   orange juice
1-1/2 t. garlic powder
1/4 t. red pepper flakes
4-oz. pkg. crumbled feta cheese

Combine tortellini, peppers, onion and olives in a large serving bowl; set aside. Combine remaining ingredients except feta cheese in a small bowl; pour over tortellini mixture. Chill for 4 to 24 hours before serving. Sprinkle with feta cheese. Serves 8.

An oh-so-easy placecard...simply write names on cards,
punch a hole in one corner and slip the hole over pear,
apple or mini pumpkin stems!

Doreen's Shrimp-Rice Salad

Doreen Matthew
San Marcos, CA

I've been making this recipe for years...it's simple to make and easily doubled or even tripled. For a special presentation, serve it on a platter lined with green or red lettuce leaves.

1 c. long-cooking rice, cooked
1 c. celery, chopped
1 c. green onion, chopped
1 lb. small shrimp, cooked and
   peeled

1 c. mayonnaise
1 T. curry powder
Optional: slivered almonds,
   toasted

Combine rice, celery, green onion and shrimp in a large bowl; set aside. Mix together mayonnaise and curry in a small bowl until well blended; stir into rice mixture. Chill for at least one hour before serving. Sprinkle with almonds, if desired. Serves 8.

Scatter pansies, buttercups or violets on serving or buffet tables...so sweet for a springtime get-together.

Chicken & Asparagus Bake

Marilyn Morel
Keene, NH

A delicious casserole that's simple to prepare
and bakes in under 45 minutes.

6 cooked chicken breasts,
   chopped
3 14-1/2 oz. cans asparagus
   pieces, drained
2-oz. jar chopped pimentos,
   drained

3/4 c. slivered almonds
3 10-3/4 oz. cans cream of
   mushroom soup
2 2.8-oz. cans French fried
   onions

Layer chicken, asparagus, pimentos, almonds and soup in a lightly
greased 2-1/2 quart casserole dish. Cover with aluminum foil; bake at
350 degrees for 30 to 40 minutes, until bubbly. Uncover and sprinkle
with onion rings; bake for an additional 5 minutes. Serves 6 to 8.

It's easy to make invitations extra-special. Simply roll up and
secure with ribbon, then, depending on the season, slip a sprig
of rosemary, bittersweet or greenery under the ribbon.

Fried Okra Salad

Lisa Martin
Tulsa, OK

*I took this dish to a ladies' function at my church and
by the time it was over, everyone had copied the recipe!*

24-oz. pkg. frozen breaded okra
10 slices bacon, crisply cooked
   and crumbled
6 roma tomatoes, chopped

1 bunch green onions, chopped
1/2 c. olive oil
1/4 c. sugar
2 T. vinegar

Fry okra according to package directions; drain. Combine okra,
bacon, tomatoes and green onions; set aside. Mix together remaining
ingredients; pour over okra mixture. Best served at room temperature.
Serves 8.

Instead of setting up one or 2 long dining tables, scatter several
smaller ones around the room so friends can chat easily.

Sweet & Tangy Punch

Jen Stout
Blandon, PA

Pour servings into tall glasses, then garnish with a lemon slice.

46-oz. can unsweetened
   pineapple juice, chilled
6-oz. can frozen lemonade
   concentrate, thawed

24-oz. bottle lemon-lime soda,
   chilled
ice cubes, crushed

Combine pineapple juice and lemonade; chill. Add soda just before
serving; serve over ice. Makes 8 to 10 servings.

Cinnamon Muffins

Lynne Brown
Reynoldsburg, OH

Perfect for enjoying with a group of friends.

1 egg, beaten
3/4 c. milk
1/2 c. butter, melted
2 c. all-purpose flour
2 t. baking powder

1 t. salt
1/2 c. brown sugar, packed
1 t. vanilla extract
2/3 c. cinnamon baking chips

Combine egg and milk in a bowl; stir well. Add butter, flour, baking
powder, salt, brown sugar and vanilla; mix until just moistened. Fold
in chips; fill greased muffin cups 3/4 full. Bake at 400 degrees for
15 to 20 minutes; remove from pan. Cool on a wire rack. Makes
10 to 12.

Life is like that…one stitch at a time taken patiently,
and the pattern will come out all right, like embroidery.
– Oliver Wendell Holmes

Fruit Salsa with Cinnamon Chips

Ashley Connelly
Louisa, VA

*I made this for our Sunday morning church refreshments
and it was a huge hit! I also like to bring this to
bridal and baby showers.*

2 kiwis, peeled and diced
2 Golden Delicious apples,
   cored, peeled and diced
1/2 lb. raspberries
16-oz. pkg. strawberries, hulled
   and diced

2 c. plus 2 T. sugar, divided
1 T. brown sugar, packed
3 T. strawberry preserves
10 10-inch flour tortillas, sliced
   into wedges
1 to 2 T. cinnamon

Combine all fruit in a large bowl; mix in 2 tablespoons sugar,
brown sugar and strawberry preserves. Cover and chill for at least
15 minutes. Mix together remaining sugar and cinnamon. Arrange
tortilla wedges on a baking sheet; coat with butter-flavored cooking
spray. Sprinkle with desired amount of cinnamon-sugar. Bake at
350 degrees for 8 to 10 minutes. Repeat with remaining tortilla
wedges; cool for 15 minutes. Serve chips with chilled fruit mixture.
Makes 10 to 15 servings.

Try topping fruity sides or salads with edible flowers...always
be sure to choose pesticide-free blooms. Some of our
favorites are pansies, violets, rose petals or nasturtiums.

Perfect Lemon Bread

*Nichole Sullivan
Santa Fe, TX*

Topped with a lemony glaze, this sweet bread is so scrumptious.

1-1/2 c. all-purpose flour
1-1/3 c. sugar, divided
1 t. baking powder
1/2 t. salt
2 eggs

1/2 c. milk
1/2 c. oil
1-1/2 t. lemon zest
4-1/2 T. lemon juice

Mix together flour, one cup sugar, baking powder and salt in a large bowl; set aside. Beat together eggs, milk, oil and zest; add to flour mixture. Stir until well blended. Pour into a greased and floured 9"x5" loaf pan. Bake at 350 degrees for 45 to 50 minutes. Combine lemon juice and remaining sugar in a small saucepan over medium heat; cook and stir until remaining sugar is dissolved. Using a skewer, poke holes in hot bread; drizzle hot glaze over top and cool. Makes one loaf.

Search out fun retro tablecloths at flea markets and tag sales... they're often found for a song. Buy a bunch, they'll bring a burst of color and whimsy to table settings!

Ladies' Lunch

Cranberry-Buttermilk Scones

Jenny Sisson
Broomfield, CO

Best enjoyed warm from the oven, topped with butter.

2 c. all-purpose flour
1/3 c. sugar
1/4 t. salt
1-1/2 t. baking powder
1/2 t. baking soda
6 T. butter

1/2 c. buttermilk
1 egg
1-1/2 t. vanilla extract
2/3 c. sweetened, dried
   cranberries

Stir first 5 ingredients together; cut in butter with a pastry blender. Combine remaining ingredients except cranberries; mix into flour mixture until just moistened. Add cranberries; drop 10 tablespoonfuls onto a greased baking sheet. Bake at 375 degrees for 15 minutes, or until golden. Makes 10.

Add warm dishes to the menu if ladies are getting together on a crisp autumn day. Fill bread bowls with soups and stews and serve up savory casseroles. Dessert can be bowls of scrumptious bread pudding and mugs of spiced cider...yum!

Mom's Cherry Soda Salad

Kym Du Pont
Grass Valley, CA

I got this recipe from my mom and it was one of the most requested at a women's salad potluck luncheon. Everyone brought a variety of gelatin salad...it was quite a rainbow on the table. This was only one of 2 that had no leftovers.

6-oz. pkg. cherry gelatin mix
2 15-oz. cans Bing cherries,
    drained and juice reserved
16-oz. can crushed pineapple,
    drained and juice reserved

12-oz. can cola, chilled
Optional: 1/2 c. chopped
    walnuts
Garnish: whipped topping

Pour gelatin mix into a large bowl; set aside. Combine reserved cherry and pineapple juices in a small saucepan over medium heat; bring to a boil. Pour over gelatin. Stir constantly until gelatin is dissolved, about 3 minutes. Add chilled cola. Refrigerate for 20 minutes. Add cherries, pineapple and walnuts, if using. Pour into a 6-cup mold. Chill for at least 4 hours, preferably overnight. To serve, unmold gelatin onto serving plate. Garnish with whipped topping. Serves 12 to 15.

Make your ladies' luncheon a recipe swap! Invite friends to choose several of their best recipes to share, then make enough copies for everyone who will be coming. It's a fun way to pass along tried & true recipes, as well as enjoy a tasty lunch.

Ladies' Lunch

Sparkling Sipper

Barb Sulser
Delaware, OH

You can also use frozen strawberries for this refreshing drink.

2 lbs. strawberries, hulled
12-oz. can frozen lemonade
   concentrate, thawed
8 t. fresh mint, chopped

8 c. crushed ice
2 c. sparkling water, chilled
Garnish: 8 hulled strawberries,
   8 sprigs fresh mint

Combine strawberries, lemonade and mint in a blender; process until smooth. Add ice; blend until smooth. Pour into glasses; top each with 1/4 cup sparkling water and stir to mix. Garnish each with a strawberry and a sprig of mint. Serve with straws for sipping. Serves 8.

Razzleberry Punch

Trisha Donley
Pinedale, WY

This is perfect for a springtime luncheon, brunch or shower.

1/2 gal. raspberry sherbet
2-ltr. bottle raspberry ginger ale,
   chilled

64-oz. bottle red fruit punch,
   chilled

Mix together all ingredients 30 minutes to one hour before serving. Refrigerate until ready to serve. Serves 25 to 30.

A brand-new watering can makes a super pitcher for punch or lemonade!

Strawberry Fruit Dip

Marsha Dixon
Bella Vista, AR

*This recipe is always a smash hit at the annual
ladies' luncheon that I have with the women of
my church...a Mothers' Day must-have.*

8-oz. pkg. strawberry-flavored
  cream cheese, softened
2 T. strawberry preserves
8-oz. container frozen whipped
  topping, thawed

7-oz. jar marshmallow creme
assorted fresh fruit, sliced

Beat together cream cheese and preserves until well blended. Fold in
whipped topping and marshmallow creme. Cover and refrigerate until
serving. Serve with fruit. Makes 4 cups.

Use Strawberry Fruit Dip for stuffed strawberries...lovely!
Cut a thin layer from the stem end of strawberries to form
a base. Starting at the opposite end of the strawberry,
make 4 cuts, being careful not to slice through the base.
Spoon or pipe dip into the center of each strawberry;
refrigerate until ready to serve.

Summertime Socials

Picnic Potato Salad

10 redskin potatoes	
1 c. mayonnaise	1 t. salt
2 T. red wine vinegar	3 green onions,
2 T. Dijon mustard	chopped
1 t. prepared horse-	3 stalks celery,
radish	chopped
2 t. sugar	1/4 c. red onion,
	chopped

Pierce potatoes several times with a fork and place in a microwave-safe dish. Microwave on high setting for 10 to 12 minutes, until firm and cooked through. Set aside to cool. In a medium bowl, whisk together mayonnaise, vinegar, mustard, horseradish, sugar and salt. Mix in green onions, celery and red onion. Slice potatoes into one-inch cubes; carefully toss with mayonnaise mixture. Refrigerate until ready to serve. Serves 10.

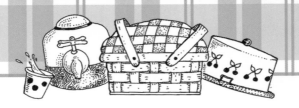

Just Perfect Sloppy Joes

Amy Wrightsel
Louisville, KY

*This recipe is very special to me. It brings back memories
of my aunt and me puttering around in the kitchen trying
to figure out just what it needed to be right.*

3 lbs. ground beef, browned
   and drained
1 onion, finely chopped
1 green pepper, chopped
28-oz. can tomato sauce
3/4 c. catsup

3 T. Worcestershire sauce
1 t. chili powder
1/2 t. pepper
1/2 t. garlic powder
8 sandwich buns, split

Combine all ingredients except sandwich buns in a slow cooker. Cover
and cook on low setting for 8 to 10 hours, or on high setting for
3 to 4 hours. Serve in sandwich buns. Serves 8.

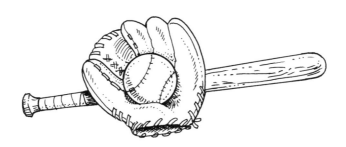

Warm-weather socials mean lots of outdoor games...
softball, sack races, tag, hide & seek and water balloon fun.
Always plan to snap some photos, so you're sure
to capture all the memories!

Mother's Fried Chicken

Evelyn Russell
Dallas, TX

This recipe was given to me by my mother 30 years ago. It is the most always asked for when I cook for church get-togethers and Sunday dinners. The first time I made this for my pastor and his wife, it brought back memories for them of their mothers' fried chicken.

4 c. self-rising flour
2 T. salt
2 T. coarse pepper

8 lbs. chicken pieces
4 to 5 c. shortening, divided

Combine flour, salt and pepper in a shallow pan. Dredge chicken in flour mixture. In a large cast-iron skillet over medium-high heat, heat 3 cups shortening to 350 degrees. Working in batches, fry chicken, covered, for about 10 minutes. Reduce heat to medium-low; fry for 30 minutes per side. Add shortening as needed. Uncover during last 5 minutes of cooking time. Drain on paper towels. Serves 8.

A wheelbarrow or wagon is just right for holding paper plates and cups along with flatware and napkins. It's easy to take right to the picnic spot and keeps picnic tables free for holding all the scrumptious food!

Bacon-Stuffed Burgers

Molly Cool
Delaware, OH

These go so fast I have to double the recipe!

4 slices bacon, crisply cooked,
crumbled and drippings
reserved
1/4 c. onion, chopped
4-oz. can mushroom pieces,
drained and diced
1 lb. ground beef

1 lb. ground pork sausage
1/4 c. grated Parmesan cheese
1/2 t. pepper
1/2 t. garlic powder
2 T. steak sauce
8 sandwich buns, split
Optional: lettuce

Heat 2 tablespoons reserved drippings in a skillet over medium heat. Add onion and sauté until tender. Add bacon and mushrooms; heat through and set aside. Combine beef, sausage, cheese, pepper, garlic powder and steak sauce in a large bowl. Shape into 16 patties. Spoon bacon mixture over 8 patties. Place remaining patties on top and press edges tightly to seal. Grill over medium coals to desired doneness. Serve on buns with lettuce, if desired. Makes 8 servings.

Invite friends to bring along flower cuttings or divided bulbs from their gardens to your next church picnic. Supply a few shovels, and in no time at all you'll have a great beginning to a friendship garden.

58

Picnic Potato Salad

Barbara Shultis
South Egremont, MA

When I bring this to our summertime picnic potluck,
I never have to worry about bringing any back home!

10 redskin potatoes
1 c. mayonnaise
2 T. red wine vinegar
2 T. Dijon mustard
1 t. prepared horseradish

2 t. sugar
1 t. salt
3 green onions, chopped
3 stalks celery, chopped
1/4 c. red onion, chopped

Pierce potatoes several times with a fork and place in a microwave-safe dish. Microwave on high setting for 10 to 12 minutes, until tender and cooked through. Set aside to cool. In a medium bowl, whisk together mayonnaise, vinegar, mustard, horseradish, sugar and salt. Mix in green onions, celery and red onion. Slice potatoes into one-inch cubes; carefully toss with mayonnaise mixture. Refrigerate until ready to serve. Serves 10.

If you find time is too short to make your own potato salad dressing, bottled coleslaw dressing is a great-tasting substitute. Add as much of the dressing as you like to potato salad ingredients, then stir gently to blend.

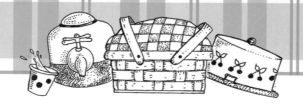

Cucumber-Onion Salad

Beverly Ray
Brandon, FL

It's just not a summertime picnic without this tangy salad.

2 cucumbers, thinly sliced
2 onions, thinly sliced
1/4 c. sugar
1 t. salt

1/4 t. pepper
1/2 to 1 c. white vinegar
1/2 c. oil

Combine all ingredients. Cover and refrigerate for 3 to 4 hours.
Serves 6 to 8.

Heavenly Deviled Eggs

Paula Barton
Kopperl, TX

A tray of these is always a big hit at every
Sunday evening fellowship.

24 eggs, hard-boiled, peeled
  and chilled
1/2 c. mayonnaise
1 t. mustard

salt and pepper to taste
Garnish: paprika, snipped fresh
  chives

Slice eggs in half and scoop yolks into a bowl. Arrange egg whites
on a serving platter; set aside. Mash yolks well with a fork. Add
mayonnaise, mustard, salt and pepper. Spoon into egg whites;
sprinkle with paprika. Chill. Makes 4 dozen.

Paper napkins that are anything but plain...just roll, slip in
plastic tableware and tie up with a cheery gingham ribbon.

Mama's Sausage & Peppers

Karen Pilcher
Burleson, TX

Back in the 1960's we had a wonderful assistant pastor, Don Giovanni Baggio, who loved to cook for all of the church events. He would say, "Let me call my mama for a real Italian recipe." Oh, how we loved him and his mama's recipes!

1/4 c. olive oil
4 lbs. Italian pork sausage links,
   cut into 1-inch pieces
2 red peppers, chopped
2 green peppers, chopped

2 onions, chopped
1 t. dried oregano
1/2 t. pepper
Optional: 8 to 10 sandwich rolls,
   split

Heat oil in a large skillet over medium heat. Add sausage and cook until browned, about 10 minutes. Remove sausage from skillet; drain. Add peppers and onions to skillet; sauté until tender, about 10 minutes. Return sausage to skillet; stir in oregano and pepper. Cook for 2 to 3 minutes, until heated through. Serve on sandwich rolls, if desired. Serves 8 to 10.

It's the sweet & simple things that mean the most...a card, a phone call or a gift from your kitchen really show you care.

Easy Southern-Style Pork Barbecue
Marilyn Morel
Keene, NH

This is known as pulled pork barbecue and is a favorite in the south. To really experience the true southern-style pork barbecue sandwich, add a generous dab of of coleslaw on the sandwich before you add the top bun. Yum!

3 to 4-lb. pork roast
1/4 c. water
2 T. smoke-flavored cooking
    sauce

pepper to taste
6 to 8 hamburger buns, split
Garnish: favorite barbecue sauce
Optional: coleslaw

Place pork roast in a slow cooker. Add water; sprinkle evenly with cooking sauce and pepper to taste. Cover and cook on low setting for 8 to 10 hours. Remove roast from slow cooker; shred meat and pull from the bone with a fork. Place meat on hamburger buns; top with barbecue sauce and a scoop of coleslaw, if desired. Makes 6 to 8 servings.

Life's sweetest joys are hidden in unsubstantial things;
an April rain, a fragrance, a vision of blue wings.
-May Riley Smith

Michelle's Best-Ever Coleslaw

Michelle Marberry
Valley, AL

*This is a must-have coleslaw at our church. It's easy
to double or triple and is a crowd pleaser every time.*

1/3 c. sugar
1/2 t. salt
1/2 c. mayonnaise
1/4 c. buttermilk
1-1/2 T. white vinegar

2-1/2 T. lemon juice
1 head cabbage, finely diced
1/4 c. carrot, peeled and finely
   diced
2 T. onion, minced

Using a blender, process first 6 ingredients until smooth; set aside.
Combine cabbage, carrot and onion in a large bowl. Add dressing and
mix well. Cover and refrigerate for several hours, or overnight. Mix
well again before serving. Serves 12.

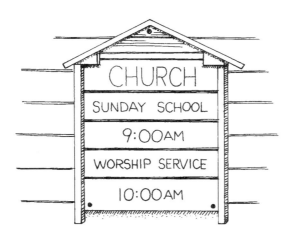

Give your favorite coleslaw recipe a fruity twist...when making
the dressing, simply substitute fruit juice for white vinegar.

Divine Chicken Salad

Jennifer Gubbins
Homewood, IL

Hearty enough to be a complete meal
when served with crusty bread.

1/4 c. white vinegar
1/4 c. dry white wine or vinegar
1 T. plus 1 t. olive oil
1 t. dried oregano
1/4 t. garlic powder
4 c. cooked fusilli or rotini pasta
1-1/2 c. cooked chicken breast, chopped
2 T. onion, finely chopped

1 T. fresh parsley, chopped
1/8 t. salt
pepper to taste
4 c. romaine lettuce, torn
2 tomatoes, chopped
16 green olives, quartered
1/4 c. crumbled feta cheese
2 T. grated Parmesan cheese

Combine vinegar, wine or vinegar, oil, oregano and garlic powder in a large bowl; whisk together until well blended. Add pasta, chicken, onion, parsley, salt and pepper; toss to mix thoroughly. Chill at least 2 hours. Add remaining ingredients at serving time; toss well and serve immediately. Makes 6 servings.

Use a melon baller to hollow out cantaloupe, honeydew or watermelon halves. The melon halves are now clever serving bowls for your tastiest chicken salad, and the juicy fruit balls will disappear quickly!

Mommy's Antipasto Salad

Yvonne Van Brimmer
Apple Valley, CA

Every time I take this to a church potluck, my bowl comes back empty! I love to make people happy with my cooking.

1 head lettuce, chopped
6-oz. can black olives, drained
1/2 lb. thick-sliced salami, quartered
2 6-oz. jars marinated artichokes, drained and coarsely chopped
1 zucchini, diced
10-oz. pkg. grape tomatoes, halved
1 green pepper, cut into strips
1 red onion, sliced into rings
6 to 8 pepperoncini, coarsely chopped
1-1/2 c. grated Parmesan cheese
16-oz. bottle Italian salad dressing
5-oz. pkg. garlic-seasoned croutons

Combine all ingredients except dressing and croutons; toss gently. Chill until serving time. Add dressing to taste; top with croutons just before serving. Serves 10.

Don't forget to bring along some kites and bubble solution when packing up your picnic goodies...simple country pleasures everyone will enjoy.

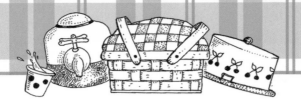

Homemade Baked Beans

Robyn Prendergast
Lynn, MA

This recipe has been passed down from my dad's side of the
family in Vermont. I make these sweet and delicious
beans in my slow cooker to keep them extra-simple.

32-oz. pkg. dried navy beans
1/2 t. baking soda
16-oz. pkg. dark brown sugar
1/4 t. ground ginger

3 to 4 c. water
1 onion, quartered
1/2 lb. salt pork, cubed

In a stockpot, cover beans with water; soak overnight. Drain beans; add fresh water to just cover beans. Stir in baking soda and bring to a boil over medium-high heat. Reduce heat; simmer for 30 minutes. In a small saucepan over medium heat, combine brown sugar and ginger. Add just enough water to cover brown sugar; cook until sugar dissolves. Place onion in a slow cooker; add beans with liquid. Stir in sugar mixture. If liquid doesn't cover beans, add just enough water to cover. Add salt pork. Cover and cook on high setting for 4 to 6 hours. Reduce to low setting; cover and cook for an additional 4 to 5 hours. Serves 10 to 12.

Mix vintage linens, set out mismatched plates and cups, hang clusters of stars and fill Mason jars with mini flag bouquets...what a grand way to celebrate the Fourth of July picnic-style.

Famous Calico Beans

*Barbara Harman
Petersburg, WV*

We have always enjoyed this recipe at church get-togethers.

1 lb. ground beef
1/4 lb. bacon, chopped
1 onion, chopped
16-oz. can pork & beans
15-oz. can kidney beans,
    drained and liquid reserved

15-oz. can butter beans, drained
    and liquid reserved
1/2 c. catsup
1/2 c. brown sugar, packed
2 T. vinegar
1/2 t. salt

Brown beef, bacon and onion in a large skillet over medium heat; drain. Spread beans in a lightly greased 13"x9" baking pan; add beef mixture. Combine catsup, brown sugar, vinegar and salt; pour over beef mixture. If more liquid is needed, add reserved liquid from beans. Bake, uncovered, at 350 degrees for one hour. Serves 8.

A roomy galvanized washtub makes a clever ice chest. Fill
a washtub with ice, juice boxes, bottles of water or soda
and they'll stay frosty all day long...it's even the perfect
watermelon cooler!

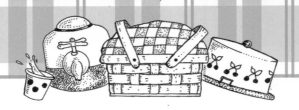

Shredded Beef Sandwiches

Sharon Beach
Potosi, MO

*I like to prepare these sandwiches for church
get-togethers because they're so tasty.*

11-1/2 oz. jar sliced
   pepperoncini
4-lb. beef chuck roast
1-3/4 t. dried basil
1-1/2 t. dried oregano
1-1/2 t. garlic powder

1-1/4 t. salt
1/4 t. pepper
1/4 c. water
1 onion, sliced
10 to 12 sandwich buns,
   split and toasted

Pour pepperoncini with liquid into a slow cooker; add roast. Mix
together spices, salt and pepper; sprinkle over meat. Add water and
onion. Cover and cook on low setting for 8 to 9 hours, until meat
is tender. Remove roast; shred using 2 forks. Return meat to slow
cooker; mix well. Using a slotted spoon, place meat on buns. Serves
10 to 12.

Have a spirited bike parade at your next social. Kids love
to decorate their bikes, and with a little crepe paper,
ribbon and imagination, you'll soon have families
cheering and kids grinning ear-to-ear.

Mother's Macaroni Salad

Kate Haney
Ellensburg, WA

A tried & true recipe with old-fashioned flavor.

8 eggs, divided
1 c. cider vinegar
1 c. water
2-1/2 c. sugar
2 T. all-purpose flour
1 T. mustard
1 t. salt

1/2 t. celery seed
1/8 t. ground ginger
2 c. mayonnaise
2 16-oz. pkgs. elbow macaroni,
  cooked
1/3 c. onion, finely chopped
2 stalks celery, chopped

Hard-boil, peel and finely chop 4 eggs; set aside. In a saucepan over low heat, combine vinegar, water, sugar, flour, mustard, seasonings and remaining eggs, beaten. Cook and stir until boiling. Remove from heat and let cool; stir in mayonnaise. Combine cooked macaroni, hard-boiled eggs, onion and celery in a large bowl; pour mixture over all. Stir well; chill until serving time. Makes 14 to 16 servings.

Church Supper
Menu:
-Macaroni Salad
- Baked Beans
-Pretzel Salad

The air is like a butterfly with frail blue wings.
The happy earth looks at the sky and sings.

–Joyce Kilmer

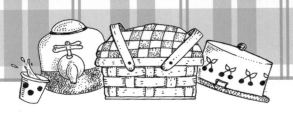

Southern Iced Tea

Anna Brown
Tahlequah, OK

I like to use decaffeinated tea...I think it tastes smoother.

4 family-size tea bags
1-1/2 c. water
1-1/2 c. sugar

ice, cubed or crushed
Garnish: lemon or orange slices,
fresh mint sprigs

Combine tea bags and water in a microwave-safe 2-cup glass container. Microwave on high setting for 7 to 8 minutes. Place sugar in a one-gallon pitcher and pour hot tea over sugar; gently squeeze excess tea from tea bags. Mix well until sugar is dissolved; add cold water to fill pitcher. Serve over ice; garnish as desired with citrus slices and mint. Makes one gallon.

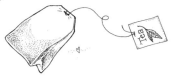

Honey-Apple Tea

Sharon Tillman
Hampton, VA

This has such a nice fruity flavor.

4 tea bags
3 c. water
1/3 c. honey

3 c. unsweetened apple juice
ice, cubed or crushed
Garnish: apple slices

Place tea bags in a heat-proof pitcher; set aside. Bring water to a boil; pour over tea bags. Let stand for 15 minutes. Discard tea bags; add honey and apple juice. Chill. Serve over ice. Serves 6 to 8.

Turn herbal tea bags into summertime sun tea. Just toss several bags into a large glass container, add water and secure the lid. Set in the sun until the tea is as strong as you'd like...simply add sugar and chill.

Summertime Socials

Buffa's Family Secret Cheese Ball

Pamela Riley
Dedham, MA

My mom gave me this recipe many years ago and it has become my specialty. At family gatherings, the first question my relatives ask me is, "Did you bring your famous cheese ball?"

8-oz. pkg. cream cheese, softened
8-oz. container refrigerated sharp pasteurized cheese spread

5-oz. jar blue cheese spread
1/2 c. butter
1/8 to 1/4 t. hot pepper sauce
1 c. chopped walnuts

Combine first 4 ingredients; mix well. Add hot pepper sauce to taste; mix again. Cover and refrigerate overnight. Shape mixture into a ball; roll in nuts. Refrigerate until ready to serve. Serves 12.

Salsa Roja

Tami Bowman
Marysville, OH

For a real treat, warm the tortilla chips.

1 lb. plum tomatoes
2 T. olive oil
5 cloves garlic, chopped
1/2 c. onion, sliced and cut into very thin strips

1/4 c. serrano chiles, chopped
1 bunch fresh cilantro, chopped
2 T. lime juice
salt to taste
tortilla chips

Arrange tomatoes on a broiler pan or a grill; roast tomatoes until skin is blackened and tomatoes are soft. Set aside to cool. Heat oil in a skillet over medium heat. Add garlic, onion and chiles; cook until golden. Place all ingredients except salt and chips in a blender and pulse to desired thickness. Stir in salt. Serve with tortilla chips. Makes about 3 cups.

Creamy Pretzel Salad

Wendy Gover
Fort Collins, CO

*Whenever I bring this to a church potluck, it's always
the first to go! This salad can be served as a side,
but is sweet enough to be served as a dessert.*

1/2 c. butter
1 c. sugar, divided
3 c. pretzels, broken
8-oz. pkg. cream cheese,
   softened

8-oz. container frozen whipped
   topping, thawed
20-oz. can pineapple tidbits,
   drained

Melt butter in a saucepan over medium heat; stir in 1/2 cup sugar
until dissolved. Place pretzels in an ungreased 13"x9" baking pan;
pour butter mixture over top. Bake at 350 degrees for 10 minutes;
let cool. Remove pretzel mixture from pan and break into pieces.
Mix together remaining sugar, cream cheese, whipped topping and
pineapple; stir in pretzel pieces. Chill. Serves 10 to 12.

Serving juicy, fruit-filled salads outdoors can sometimes be
tricky, so why not spoon individual servings into one-pint,
wide-mouth Mason jars? Secure the lids, and when it's serving
time, friends will find the tasty fruit salad, and the juices,
stay right inside the jars!

Marsha's Cheery Cherry Salad

Amy Smith
Las Vegas, NV

This was one of my mother's favorite recipes. She was very involved in her church and loved to take this refreshing salad to get-togethers.

15-oz. can tart cherries, drained
   and juice reserved
8-1/2 oz. can crushed
   pineapple, drained and
   juice reserved

1/2 c. sugar
2 3-oz. pkgs. cherry gelatin mix
1-1/2 c. ginger ale
Optional: 1/2 c. chopped pecans

Pour reserved cherry and pineapple juices into a 2-cup measuring cup. Add enough water to equal 1-3/4 cups. Pour into a small saucepan and add sugar. Bring to a boil over medium heat; stir in gelatin. Remove from heat; add fruit and ginger ale. Pour into a large serving bowl; chill in refrigerator until thickened, but not completely set. Stir in pecans, if desired. Return to refrigerator until fully set. Serves 6 to 8.

Mom's Tropical Salad

Bobbie Kendall
McDonough, GA

Great for any summer church picnic! My mother has been making this for 40 years.

1 c. mandarin oranges, drained
1 c. pineapple chunks, drained
1 c. mini marshmallows
1 c. sweetened flaked coconut

8-oz. container sour cream
Optional: halved maraschino
   cherries, chopped pecans

In a bowl, mix together all ingredients except cherries and pecans; refrigerate overnight. Top with maraschino cherries and nuts, if desired. Serves 10.

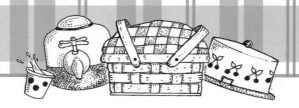

Zesty Corn Salsa

Connie Fortune
Covington, OH

This is a sure crowd-pleaser at picnics and potlucks!

2 c. frozen corn, thawed
1/4 c. red pepper, chopped
2 green onions, sliced
1 jalapeño pepper, halved,
   seeded and chopped

1 T. fresh cilantro, chopped
2 T. lime juice
1 T. oil
1/4 to 1/2 t. salt
corn chips

Combine all ingredients except corn chips; mix well. Cover; refrigerate for one hour, or until well chilled. Serve with corn chips. Makes 2-1/2 cups.

3-Corn Casserole

Kim Allmon
Chesterton, IN

If I don't bring this to our church suppers, numerous people will ask me where it is and why I didn't make it!

14-3/4 oz. can creamed corn
15-1/4 oz. can corn, drained
8-1/2 oz. pkg. corn muffin mix

8-oz. container sour cream
1/2 c. butter, melted

Combine all ingredients; pour into a greased 2-quart casserole dish. Bake, uncovered, at 350 degrees for one hour, until center is set and top is golden. Serves 8.

Summertime whimsies...retro metal picnic baskets and kids' sand pails make terrific ice buckets and napkin holders.

Hot German Potato Salad

Rogene Rogers
Bemidji, MN

I found this recipe years ago in an old German cookbook and it's been a success at every church function I have made it for.

6 potatoes
1 lb. bacon, diced, crisply
    cooked and drippings
    reserved
1-1/2 c. onion, chopped

1 c. plus 2 T. vinegar
1-1/2 T. sugar
1-1/2 t. salt
1/4 t. pepper

Cover potatoes with water in a saucepan; bring to a boil over medium heat. Simmer for 20 minutes, or until tender; drain. Peel and cut into 1/4-inch slices; place in a large serving bowl and set aside. Heat 6 tablespoons reserved drippings in a large skillet; discard any remaining drippings. Add onion to skillet; sauté until translucent, stirring occasionally. Stir in vinegar, sugar, salt and pepper; bring to a boil. Add bacon, stirring to mix well. Pour hot mixture over potato slices; toss lightly to coat evenly. Serve warm. Serves 12.

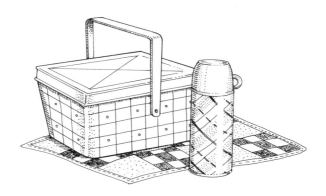

Happiness is like potato salad…
when shared with others, it's a picnic!
–Unknown

Papa's Italian Sandwiches

Geneva Rogers
Gillette, WY

A really tasty sandwich! Keep cooked sausages with sauce mixture separate from rolls and cheese, then assemble sandwiches when you arrive at your picnic spot.

24 Italian pork sausage links
5 green peppers, thinly sliced
1 onion, chopped
12-oz. can tomato paste
15-oz. can tomato sauce
1 c. water
1 T. sugar

5 cloves garlic, minced
1 T. dried basil
1-1/4 t. dried oregano
1 t. salt
24 hoagie rolls, split
Garnish: grated Parmesan
    cheese

Brown 6 to 8 sausages at a time in a large Dutch oven over medium heat. Repeat with remaining sausages. Drain sausages and set aside, reserving 3 tablespoons drippings in Dutch oven. Add peppers and onions. Sauté until crisp-tender; drain. Stir in tomato paste, sauce, water, sugar, garlic, herbs and salt. Add sausages; bring to a boil over medium heat. Reduce heat; simmer, covered, for 30 to 45 minutes. Serve on rolls; sprinkle with cheese. Makes 24 servings.

If you're preparing sandwiches before a picnic, slip them into wax paper bags and arrange open-end up in a vintage picnic tin. The bags mean less mess, making it so much easier for little hands to hold.

Windy City Kraut Dogs

Tori Willis
Champaign, IL

Along with chili dogs and cheese dogs,
these are a summertime favorite.

1/2 to 3/4 c. Thousand Island
    salad dressing
3/4 c. sauerkraut, drained
3 slices bacon, crisply cooked
    and crumbled

8 hot dogs
8 hot dog buns, split and
    toasted

Combine salad dressing, sauerkraut and bacon; set aside. Place hot dogs on a medium-hot grill; cook until done. Place hot dogs in buns; spoon dressing mixture over top. Makes 8 servings.

Michigan Sauce for Hot Dogs

Laureen White
Woodstock, VA

Tote the slow cooker to your picnic...this sauce won't last long!

2 lbs. ground beef
8-oz. can tomato sauce
2 T. mustard

2 T. chili powder
1 T. sugar

Mix all ingredients together in a slow cooker. Cover and cook on low setting for 8 to 10 hours. Makes about 5 cups.

A vintage-style wire egg basket with its swinging handle
makes it easy to carry all kinds of picnic foods. Line
the basket with a tea towel, then add potato chips,
dinner rolls, buns, pretzels or corn chips.

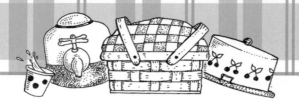

Jane's Strawberry-Rhubarb Pie

Regina Gill
Coatesville, PA

My friend, Jane Krueger, loved strawberry-rhubarb pie. As we visited together after her auto accident, she mentioned a craving for this pie. I told her if she shared her recipe, I would make it for her...when I did, she said it was the best! Although she is no longer with us, I share this recipe in her memory.

1/2 c. sugar
1/4 c. quick-cooking tapioca, uncooked
1/8 t. salt
2 c. strawberries, hulled and halved

2 c. rhubarb, cut into 1-inch pieces
Optional: zest of 1 orange
9-inch pie crust
2 T. butter, diced

Combine sugar, tapioca and salt in a large bowl. Add fruit and zest, if using; toss to coat. Spoon into pie crust; dot with butter. Bake at 400 degrees for 20 minutes. Reduce heat to 350 degrees; bake for an additional 20 to 25 minutes. Serves 8.

For a new twist, spoon pie servings into pretty parfait cups and top with dollops of whipped cream.

Peaches & Cream Pie

Lori Ritchey
Denver, PA

My mom, who is a pastor's wife, made this pie when I was growing up. Now I am a pastor's wife and make this delicious pie too!

3/4 c. all-purpose flour
1 t. baking powder
1/2 t. salt
3-oz. pkg. cook & serve
   vanilla pudding mix
3 T. butter, softened
1 egg
1/2 c. milk

16-oz. can sliced peaches,
   drained and 5 T. juice
   reserved
8-oz. pkg. cream cheese,
   softened
1/2 c. sugar
Garnish: cinnamon-sugar
   to taste

Combine first 7 ingredients in a large bowl; beat with an electric mixer for 2 minutes. Pour into a greased 9" pie plate. Arrange peach slices on top; set aside. Beat together cream cheese, sugar and reserved juice for 2 minutes. Spoon over peaches; sprinkle with cinnamon-sugar. Bake at 350 degrees for 30 minutes. Serves 8.

For a super-easy summertime treat, fill an enamelware pail with crushed ice and lots of fresh fruit. Picnic perfect because it's easy to tote and the fruit stays nice and chilled.

Lemon Trifle

Nancy Girard
Chesapeake, VA

Wonderful for a summer meal when you want a special dessert!

14-oz. can sweetened
 condensed milk
8-oz. container lemon yogurt
1 T. lemon zest
8-oz. container frozen whipped
 topping, thawed
1 angel food cake, cut into bite-
 size pieces

1/3 c. lemon juice
2 c. strawberries, hulled and
 sliced
1 c. blueberries
1 c. raspberries
1/2 c. sweetened flaked coconut,
 lightly toasted

Combine first 3 ingredients in a mixing bowl; fold in whipped topping. Toss angel food cake cubes and lemon juice together. Layer 1/3 of cake cubes in a trifle bowl. Spoon 1/3 condensed milk mixture over cake; top with strawberries. Layer 1/3 of remaining cake cubes over strawberries, 1/3 of condensed milk mixture and blueberries. Repeat with remaining cake, condensed milk mixture and raspberries. Sprinkle with coconut. Cover and chill for at least 8 hours. Serves 8.

Enjoy the fun of an old-fashioned pie or cake auction!
Bidding on sweet treats made by the youth group
is a terrific fundraiser for summer camp.

Texas Sheet Cake

April Allen
Surprise, AZ

A friend from church made this for a reception at my home and it is wonderful! It serves lots of people and is a chocolate lover's dream.

2 c. sugar
2 c. all-purpose flour
1/4 c. baking cocoa
1 c. butter
1 c. water

2 eggs
1/2 c. buttermilk
1 t. baking soda
1 t. vanilla extract
1/2 t. cinnamon

Combine sugar, flour and baking cocoa in a large bowl; set aside. Combine butter and water in a saucepan; bring to a boil over medium heat. Add to dry ingredients. In a separate bowl, beat together eggs, buttermilk, baking soda, vanilla and cinnamon until well mixed; add to cocoa mixture. Pour into a greased 15"x10" jelly-roll pan. Bake at 350 degrees for 30 minutes. Spread warm frosting over top. Serves 24.

Frosting:

1/2 c. butter, melted
6 T. milk
1 c. mini marshmallows
2 T. baking cocoa

1 t. vanilla extract
2 c. powdered sugar
1 c. chopped pecans

Combine butter, milk, marshmallows and cocoa in a saucepan over medium heat; bring to a boil. Add remaining ingredients, mixing well. Remove from heat and quickly spread over cake.

Sweet & Simple Lemonade

Zoe Bennett
Columbia, SC

As easy as 1-2-3, there's nothing like real lemonade.

1 c. lemon juice
1/2 c. superfine sugar

4 c. water
ice, cubed or crushed

Combine lemon juice and sugar in a pitcher; stir until dissolved. Add cold water, mixing well. Serve over ice. Makes 5 servings.

Homemade Root Beer

Lynn Williams
Muncie, IN

Always wear gloves when handling the dry ice. Keep in mind not to seal the container tightly after adding the dry ice as it makes the pressure build up inside.

4 lbs. sugar
4 gal. water

2-oz. bottle root beer
concentrate
4 lbs. dry ice

Combine sugar, water and root beer concentrate in a large clear plastic container. Add dry ice; cover loosely. Let stand for 45 minutes to one hour. Serve immediately or store in an airtight container. Makes 4 gallons.

It's easy to keep pesky bugs away from pitchers of root beer or lemonade... simply stitch buttons or charms to the edges of tea towels and drape over the pitchers.

Snacks & Such...
fun food for kids

Celebration Cake Cones

18-1/2 oz. pkg.
  favorite cake mix
1/2 c. plus 3 T.
  water
2 eggs
1 t. vanilla extract

1 T. oil
24 flat-bottomed ice
  cream cones
Garnish: frosting,
  candy sprinkles

Combine cake mix and 1/2 cup water; beat for
one minute. Add eggs, remaining water, vanilla
and oil, mix well. Wrap aluminum foil around
bottom of cones; place in muffin cups. Fill each
cone 1/2 full with batter. Bake at 400 degrees
for 15 minutes, or until cake springs back when
touched. Cool completely; decorate as desired.

7-League Pizza Burger

Thomas Richardson
Marinette, WI

Your little All-Stars will love this!

1 lb. ground beef
1/3 c. grated Parmesan cheese
6-oz. can tomato paste
1 t. dried oregano
1 t. salt
1/8 t. pepper
1 loaf French bread, halved
   lengthwise

1/4 c. sliced black olives
3 tomatoes, peeled and thinly
   sliced
5 slices sharp pasteurized
   process cheese
1/4 c. onion, finely chopped

Combine ground beef, cheese, tomato paste, oregano, salt and pepper. Spread evenly onto both bread halves. Broil about 5 inches from heat source for 12 minutes, or until meat is done. Arrange tomato and cheese slices alternately down the center of each half. Broil for an additional one to 2 minutes, until cheese starts to melt. Slice each half into 4 to 5 pieces. Makes 5 servings.

The promise of a savory 7-League Pizza Burger is all it takes to get kids motivated for a service project! The little time it takes to help weed a neighbor's garden or plant flowers around the chapel pays big rewards...kids learn to give of their time and care for others.

Snacks & Such...
fun food for kids

Chili Crescent Cheese Dogs

Jen Martineau
Delaware, OH

So easy to make, the kids will love to help out!

8-oz. tube refrigerated
   crescent rolls
8 hot dogs

1 c. shredded Cheddar cheese
1 c. chili

Separate crescent rolls into individual pieces. Place a hot dog in middle of each dough triangle; sprinkle with cheese. Spoon chili over cheese. Fold dough corners inward to partially cover hot dog, pressing ends to seal. Arrange hot dogs on an ungreased baking sheet. Bake at 425 degrees for 10 to 12 minutes, until crescents are golden and hot dogs are heated through. Serves 8.

Mom's Famous Macaroni & Cheese

Sonja Wilsey
Alachua, FL

This recipe is the best macaroni & cheese I have ever eaten! The recipe was given to me by my mother, Bessie Wilson, who has been preparing this dish for 60 years. It is always a must-have for her children, grandchildren and great-grandchildren.

8-oz. pkg. elbow macaroni,
   cooked
6 T. margarine, softened
5-oz. can evaporated milk

1 c. milk
2 eggs, beaten
12-oz. pkg. shredded Cheddar
   cheese, divided

Combine macaroni, margarine, milks, eggs and 2 cups shredded cheese; mix well. Pour into a greased 13"x9" baking pan; top with remaining cheese. Bake at 350 degrees for 30 minutes. Makes 8 to 10 servings.

Chicken Nibbles

Kelly Alderson
Erie, PA

Kids will flock to these yummy, miniature drumsticks.

2/3 c. potato chips, crushed
1/2 t. chili powder
1/4 t. onion powder
1/8 t. pepper

16 chicken drummettes,
   skin removed
2 T. butter, melted

Combine potato chips, chili powder, onion powder and pepper on a sheet of wax paper. Dip chicken in melted butter; roll in potato chip mixture. Arrange on a lightly greased baking sheet. Broil 3 inches from heat for 3 minutes. Turn and broil for an additional 3 to 5 minutes. Serves 6 to 8.

Patsy's First-Place Gelatin Salad

Patsy Ball
Marlow, OK

This recipe was requested by our youth during the Summer Church Camp. It was entered and won first place in the Church Camp Cooks contest!

8-oz. can crushed pineapple
3-oz. pkg. lemon gelatin mix
8-oz. pkg. cream cheese,
   softened
2-oz. jar diced pimentos,
   drained

3/4 c. celery, chopped
3/4 c. chopped pecans
1 c. frozen whipped topping,
   thawed

Combine pineapple and gelatin mix in a saucepan over medium heat; heat until boiling and gelatin is dissolved. Remove; let cool. Mix together remaining ingredients except whipped topping; stir into pineapple mixture. Stir in whipped topping and spoon into a serving bowl. Refrigerate until set. Serves 10 to 15.

Roepke Family Casserole

Dana Roepke
Midland, TX

*This is one of my family's favorites. My youngest daughter
began making this when she was 7. She divides it into
2 casseroles, one for her grandparents and one for us!*

1-1/2 lbs. ground beef
1 c. onion, chopped
15-1/4 oz. can corn, drained
10-3/4 oz. can cream of chicken
   soup
10-3/4 oz. can cream of
   mushroom soup

8-oz. container sour cream
3/4 t. salt
1/4 t. pepper
3 c. cooked extra wide egg
   noodles
1 c. bread crumbs
3 T. butter, melted

Brown ground beef in a large skillet over medium heat; add onion.
Cook until tender; drain. Add corn, soups, sour cream, salt and pepper.
Stir in noodles; spoon into a lightly greased 4-quart casserole dish.
Combine bread crumbs and melted butter in a small bowl; sprinkle
over top. Bake, uncovered, at 350 degrees for 30 minutes, or until
golden. Serves 8 to 10.

If your church has an annual conference, casseroles like
Roepke Family Casserole are kid-friendly and so nice
for sharing with families between sessions.

Super Simple Tacos

Dale Duncan
Waterloo, IA

Kids love to build their own tacos!

16-oz. can refried beans
1/2 c. salsa
8 corn taco shells, warmed

1 c. shredded Cheddar cheese
1 c. lettuce, shredded
1 tomato, finely chopped

Combine beans and salsa in a small saucepan over medium heat. Cook for 2 to 3 minutes until heated through, stirring frequently. Fill taco shells with bean mixture. Top with cheese, lettuce and tomato. Serves 4.

Turn your budding chefs loose in the kitchen! Get a group of kids together to whip up a quick & easy meal like Super Simple Tacos. Not only is it a great way to teach kids some cooking basics, they'll have a ball cooking with friends.

Crispy Chicken Bites

Amanda Lusignolo
Columbus, OH

Bite-size nuggets of crispy chicken...
just right for little hands to hold on to.

1-1/2 c. corn flake cereal,
   crushed
1 t. paprika
1/2 t. Italian seasoning
1/4 t. garlic powder
1/4 t. onion powder
salt and pepper to taste

1/2 c. milk
2 boneless, skinless chicken
   breasts, cut into 2-inch
   pieces
1/4 c. butter, melted
Garnish: favorite dipping sauce

Combine cereal and seasonings in a shallow bowl; set aside. Pour milk into a separate bowl. Dip chicken pieces into milk, then into crumbs and coat thoroughly. Place in single layer on a baking sheet sprayed with non-stick vegetable spray. Drizzle butter over chicken, sprinkle with additional salt, if desired. Bake at 350 degrees for 15 to 20 minutes, or until no longer pink in the middle. Serve with your favorite sauce. Serves 4.

Crispy Chicken Bites are always a popular food. Give 'em a twist...after dipping chicken pieces in milk, roll in crushed potato chips. Try sour cream & onion or BBQ for a real flavor boost!

Parmesan Fish Sticks

Wendy Jacobs
Idaho Falls, ID

*Round out this sea-worthy lunch with
a side of fish-shaped crackers!*

2 eggs
2 T. water
salt and pepper to taste
1-1/2 c. seasoned dry bread
   crumbs
3 T. grated Parmesan cheese

2 lbs. fillet of sole, sliced into
   4"x2" sticks
1/4 c. olive oil
Optional: lemon wedges,
   tartar sauce

Beat together eggs, water, salt and pepper in a small bowl; set aside.
Combine bread crumbs and Parmesan cheese in a shallow bowl.
Dip fish sticks into egg mixture; dredge in bread crumbs. Heat oil in
a large skillet over medium-high heat. Add fish; cook until golden,
about 3 minutes per side. Drain on paper towels. Serve with lemon
wedges and tartar sauce, if desired. Serves 6.

Serve up Parmesan Fish Sticks in a brand new sand pail...
go all out and enjoy a silly game of Go Fish afterward!

A-B-C Chicken Soup

Melanie Lowe
Dover, DE

*Who can resist the fun of spelling out
names with alphabet soup?*

2 t. oil
1/2 lb. boneless, skinless
   chicken breast
3 c. chicken broth
3 c. tomato juice
3/4 c. water

1/4 t. dried oregano
1 t. Worcestershire sauce
10-oz. pkg. frozen mixed
   vegetables
2/3 c. alphabet macaroni,
   uncooked

Heat oil in a Dutch oven over medium-high heat. Add chicken; cook, stirring often, for about 3 minutes. Add broth, tomato juice, water, oregano and Worcestershire sauce. Bring to a boil; add vegetables and macaroni. Reduce heat; simmer for 8 to 10 minutes, until vegetables and macaroni are tender. Serves 6.

Plan a pioneer trek this summer! Show the kids how life was on the trail west and about their ancestors too...a great teaching opportunity. End the day around the campfire with a homemade pot of A-B-C Chicken Soup and campfire songs.

Fiesta Casserole

Barbara Boyle
Sunbury, PA

Serve up this tasty casserole with a variety of colorful tortilla chips. Tortilla chips can be found in yellow, orange, red and blue.

16-oz. pkg. elbow macaroni, uncooked
1/4 c. butter
1/4 c. grated Parmesan cheese
1/2 t. Italian seasoning
1/4 t. salt

2 eggs, beaten
2 15-oz. cans pizza sauce
8-oz. pkg. shredded mozzarella cheese
favorite pizza toppings

Cook macaroni in a large pot of boiling water for 8 minutes; rinse with hot water and return to pot. Add butter; stir until melted. Stir in Parmesan cheese, Italian seasoning and salt; mix well. Add eggs, blending well; pour into a greased 15"x10" jelly-roll pan. Bake at 350 degrees for 10 minutes; remove from oven and add pizza sauce, shredded cheese and your favorite pizza toppings. Bake for an additional 20 minutes, or until cheese is bubbly. Serves 6 to 8.

We find...delight in the beauty and happiness of children that makes the heart too big for the body.

–Ralph Waldo Emerson

Easy-as-Pie Cheeseburger Bake

Beverly Liles
Roseboro, NC

This recipe was one way I could always be assured that my youngest daughter would eat. It combines 2 favorites...meat & potatoes. I love it when I'm asked to make this for church socials. Now it's a favorite of my minister and his wife.

3 lbs. ground beef, browned
   and drained
15-oz. can tomato sauce
1/4 c. barbecue sauce
salt and pepper to taste

2 9-inch deep-dish pie crusts,
   baked
4 c. mashed potatoes
1-1/2 c. shredded Cheddar
   cheese

Combine ground beef, tomato sauce, barbecue sauce, salt and pepper in a large bowl; mix well. Divide beef mixture evenly into pie crusts. Spread mashed potatoes over both pies, smoothing edges to seal. Sprinkle with cheese. Bake, uncovered, at 350 degrees for 15 to 20 minutes. Let stand for 15 minutes before slicing. Makes 2 pies, 4 servings each.

When kids get together, it's a good idea to have some games in mind. Pin the Tail on the Donkey and face painting are fun for little ones, while a game of softball or water balloon volleyball is sure to be a hit with the teenagers.

Tortilla Triangles

Beverly Ray
Brandon, FL

Little ones will love learning their shapes when you serve these!

8-oz. pkg. cream cheese,
   softened
1/2 c. sour cream
4-oz. can chopped green chiles
1/4 c. green onion, chopped

Optional: 1 t. jalapeño pepper,
   chopped
salt and pepper to taste
10 8-inch flour tortillas
Garnish: salsa

Combine all ingredients except tortillas and salsa; mix well. Spread mixture equally onto 5 tortillas. Stack all tortillas on top of each other. Repeat with remaining filling and tortillas. Wrap in plastic wrap; chill in refrigerator for at least 4 hours. Slice into wedges. Chill until ready to serve. Serve with salsa. Makes about 16 servings.

Tortilla Triangles are just the thing when you're looking for a quick-to-fix snack. Shake up the taste by adding shredded cheese or guacamole before layering. Olé!

My-Oh-My Pizza Pie

Sherry Gordon
Arlington Heights, IL

Mini pizzas that are so easy to make.

8-oz. can pizza sauce
4 English muffins, split
   and toasted

1/2 c. deli ham, chopped
1/2 c. green pepper, chopped
1 c. shredded mozzarella cheese

Spread pizza sauce on muffins. Top with ham and green pepper; sprinkle with cheese. Broil for 3 minutes, or until heated through and cheese is melted. Makes 8.

Pin the pepperoni on the pizza? Sure! An oh-so clever idea sure to keep little ones busy while homemade pizza is baking away in the oven.

Pretzel Twists

Marlene Darnell
Newport Beach, CA

Twist the soft pretzel dough into letters and numbers!

2 16-oz. loaves frozen bread
   dough, thawed
1 egg white, beaten

1 t. water
coarse salt to taste

Divide dough into twenty-four, 1-1/2 inch balls. Roll each ball into a rope 14-1/2 inches long. Shape into numbers or letters; arrange one inch apart on lightly greased baking sheets. Let stand for 20 minutes. Whisk together egg white and water; brush over pretzels. Sprinkle with salt. Place a shallow pan with one inch of boiling water on bottom rack of oven. Bake pretzels on rack above water at 350 degrees for 20 minutes, or until golden. Makes 2 dozen.

It's easy to give soft pretzels a new flavor. Simply sprinkle them with cinnamon-sugar, drizzle with powdered sugar icing or dust with garlic powder,

Wiggly Gummies

Heidi Jakubiak
Chrisman, IL

We have lots of fun making these...the kids love 'em. You might even want to make them in silly shaped candy molds.

1 c. boiling water	2 .03-oz. envs. favorite-flavor
2 3-oz. envs. favorite-flavor	sugar-free drink mix
sugar-free gelatin mix	3 1-oz. envs. unflavored gelatin

Combine boiling water and remaining ingredients. Pour into a lightly greased 8"x8" baking pan; cover and chill for 2 to 3 hours, until completely set. Cut into 1/4-inch strips to form "worms." Makes about 2-1/2 dozen.

Kid fun...laminate comic strips from the newspaper for placemats or napkin rings!

Dad's Caramel Popcorn

Alissa Post
New York, NY

*I have fond memories of helping my dad make batch
after batch of this for church camping trips and socials.*

1 c. butter
2 c. brown sugar, packed
1/2 c. light corn syrup
1 t. salt

1/2 t. baking soda
1 t. vanilla extract
6 qts. popped popcorn

Melt butter in a saucepan over medium heat. Stir in brown sugar,
corn syrup and salt. Bring to a boil, stirring constantly. Boil for
5 minutes without stirring; remove from heat. Add baking soda
and vanilla; mix well. Place popcorn in an extra-large bowl; pour
mixture over popcorn, stirring to coat well. Spread popcorn on lightly
greased baking sheets. Bake at 250 degrees for 15 minutes. Stir; bake
for an additional 15 minutes. Cool; store in an airtight container.
Serves 16 to 20.

A summertime car wash is a favorite fundraiser. Bring along
some snacks, bottled water and fresh fruit to
keep the kids' energy up.

Cocoa Drops

Patsy Ball
Marlow, OK

These were made for the youth at our church camp. After the first batch was inhaled, a very sweet little boy asked me if I could please make more. During the week I made 10 more batches and the little boy gave me a big hug and told me how much he appreciated me making these for all the kids.

1 c. sugar
1/2 c. light corn syrup
1/4 c. honey

1 c. creamy peanut butter
6 c. chocolate puffed corn cereal

Combine sugar, syrup and honey in a saucepan over medium heat; bring to a rolling boil. Remove from heat. Stir in peanut butter, mixing well. Stir in cereal. Drop by tablespoonfuls onto wax paper; let stand until firm. Store in an airtight container. Makes 3 dozen.

Church camp is a summer activity kids always look forward to. Whip up some bite-size cookies or snack mix and spoon into new sports bottles...they make snacks so easy to tote on hikes or canoe trips.

Supreme Cheesecake Dip

Patricia Walker
Mocksville, NC

Make the serving bowl for this dip kid-friendly and fun. Spoon it into orange or melon halves, or even into a sundae cup.

2 8-oz. pkgs. cream cheese,
    softened
1/2 c. frozen strawberries,
    thawed and drained
1/4 c. sugar

1/4 c. sour cream
1-1/2 t. vanilla extract
graham crackers
fresh fruit

Combine cream cheese, strawberries, sugar, sour cream and vanilla in a blender. Process until very smooth; chill for at least 2 hours. Serve with graham crackers and fresh fruit for dipping. Makes about 3 cups.

The supreme happiness of life
is the conviction that we are loved.

–Victor Hugo

Rocky Road Frozen Sandwiches

Stacie Avner
Delaware, OH

A snap to prepare...you can have a frosty treat anytime!

1 c. chocolate frosting
1/2 c. mini marshmallows
32 graham cracker squares,
   divided

1/2 c. marshmallow creme
1/2 gal. chocolate ice cream,
   softened

Mix together frosting and marshmallows; spread over half of graham crackers. Spread marshmallow creme over remaining graham crackers. Spread 1/2 cup ice cream onto graham crackers coated with frosting mixture. Top with remaining graham crackers. Wrap individually in plastic wrap and freeze until firm. Makes 16.

An ice cream social is made for kids big or little!
So easy to plan, it's a get-together kids of all ages
can set up and enjoy with family & friends.

Cookie Marshmallow Bars

Amy Bishop
Southington, CT

My favorite Sunday school teacher always made these
for me because she knew how much I loved them!

30 chocolate chip cookies,
   divided
1/4 c. butter, melted

7-oz. jar marshmallow creme
1/4 c. chopped peanuts

Coarsely chop 8 cookies; set aside. Finely crush remaining cookies.
Mix together crushed cookies and butter. Press mixture into a greased
9"x9" baking pan. Top evenly with dollops of marshmallow creme,
leaving 1/2-inch border around all sides. Sprinkle with peanuts and
chopped cookies. Bake at 350 degrees for 15 minutes, just until
marshmallow creme begins to turn golden. Cool completely in pan on
wire rack. Makes 20.

A plate of cookies is a sweet way to say "Thanks!" to
a youth leader...it shows how much you
appreciate her talents and time.

Cheer-'em-On Fruit Pizza

Debra Renner
Romeo, MI

I would make this recipe for every girls' volleyball tournament game my daughter played in. Both the boys and girls who came to cheer on her team loved it...trust me, it won't last long!

2 18-oz. tubes refrigerated
　 sugar cookie dough
8-oz. pkg. cream cheese,
　 softened
3/4 c. powdered sugar

12-oz. container frozen whipped
　 topping, thawed
Garnish: sliced strawberries,
　 sliced kiwi, blueberries

Spread cookie dough onto a lightly greased 15"x10" jelly-roll pan. Bake at 375 degrees for 10 to 15 minutes, until lightly golden; cool. Combine cream cheese, powdered sugar and whipped topping; spread over baked crust. Top with favorite fruit. Makes 12 servings.

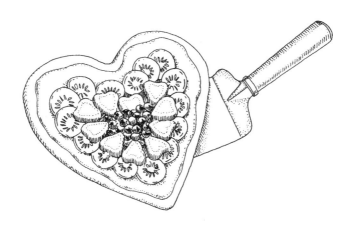

Make your Fruit Pizza heart-shaped...what better way to show the kids you care?

Chocolate Chip Cookie Dessert

Kim Allmon
Chesterton, IN

*This is a quick & easy dessert that always disappears first
at any of our church potluck dinners. Not only is this
a hit with the kids, it also is tops with adults!*

16-oz. pkg. crunchy chocolate
   chip cookies
milk for dipping

8-oz. container frozen whipped
   topping, thawed
Garnish: chocolate curls

Quickly dip cookies into milk; arrange in an ungreased 13"x9" baking
pan. Spread a layer of whipped topping over cookies. Repeat layers,
ending with whipped topping. Garnish with chocolate curls. Refrigerate
overnight. Serves 15 to 20.

Cookie cutters make the prettiest lollipop cakes, and they're
so easy. Simply use a cookie cutter to cut out shapes from
cake slices. Frost cut-outs, then insert an ice cream stick
into the side of each...done!

Dreamy Orange Pie

Traci Bendele
Ann Arbor, MI

My husband can just about devour this pie in one sitting! I also have made this in an 8"x8" baking pan and sliced it into bars.

2 c. gingersnap cookies, crushed
1/4 c. chopped pecans
1/4 c. butter, melted
1 qt. orange sherbet, softened

1 to 1-1/2 c. vanilla ice cream, softened
8-oz. container frozen whipped topping, thawed

Mix together cookie crumbs, pecans and melted butter; press into an ungreased 9" deep-dish pie plate. Spread 1/3 of the sherbet over crust; spread 1/3 of the ice cream over sherbet. Repeat layers; freeze for 2 to 3 hours. Let stand at room temperature for 15 to 20 minutes before serving. Spread whipped topping over top. Serves 8 to 10.

Hosting a carnival for the little ones? Slices of
Dreamy Orange Pie will go quickly at the dessert booth!

Ice Cream Delight

Kristen Oudshoorn
Ridgely, MD

*This is really easy to prepare and as the
name says, an absolute delight!*

12 ice cream sandwiches
6-1/2 oz. can chocolate-flavored
   whipped topping

12-oz. pkg. malted milk balls,
   crushed

Arrange 4 ice cream sandwiches side-by-side on a serving platter.
Spread a layer of whipped topping over sandwiches. Sprinkle with
1/3 of crushed candy. Repeat layers, ending with crushed candy.
Freeze for 3 hours. Serves 8 to 10.

Bring along bottles of root beer and red pop to the ice cream
social for the best floats…don't forget the twisty straws!

2-4-8 Peanut Butter Cookies

Sharon Velenosi
Garden Grove, CA

This recipe makes enough for all of the Sunday school classes!

4 c. margarine, softened
4 c. sugar
4 c. brown sugar, packed
8 eggs
4 c. creamy peanut butter

4 t. vanilla extract
8 c. all-purpose flour
4 t. baking soda
2 t. salt

Mix together margarine and sugars in a large bowl. Add eggs, one at a time, beating well after each addition. Mix in peanut butter; add vanilla. Combine remaining ingredients in a large bowl; gradually add to margarine mixture. Drop by teaspoonfuls onto lightly greased baking sheets. Flatten with a fork dipped in sugar. Bake at 350 degrees for 10 minutes. Makes 30 dozen.

Recipes like 2-4-8 Peanut Butter Cookies are just what you'll need when planning a youth bake sale. A chocolate star, mini peanut butter cup or chocolate drop added to the center before baking makes them irresistible!

Celebration Cake Cones

Arlene Price
Mehoopany, PA

Now these will get raves!

18-1/2 oz. pkg. favorite
   cake mix
1/2 c. plus 3 T. water
2 eggs
1 t. vanilla extract

1 T. oil
24 flat-bottomed ice cream
   cones
Garnish: frosting, candy
   sprinkles

Combine cake mix and 1/2 cup water; beat for one minute. Add eggs, remaining water, vanilla and oil; mix well. Wrap aluminum foil around bottoms of cones; place in muffin cups. Fill each cone 1/2 full with batter. Bake at 400 degrees for 15 minutes, or until cake springs back when touched. Cool completely; decorate as desired. Makes 24.

Use your favorite flavor of lollipop
as a stir stick in a fizzy soda!

Election Day Dinners

Slow-Cooker Cola Ham

| 1/2 c. brown sugar, packed | 12-oz. can cola |
| 1 t. dry mustard | 3 to 4-lb. fully-cooked ham |

Combine brown sugar and mustard; add enough cola to make a glaze consistency and set aside. Place ham in slow cooker; pour glaze over top, coating well. Cover and cook on low setting for 8 to 10 hours, basting occasionally with juices. Serves 8 to 10.

Julie's Chicken Pie

Julie Zahn
Syracuse, NE

*This recipe is a crowd pleaser! Whether served at
a social event or at home, it always disappears.*

4 c. cooked chicken, cubed
10-3/4 oz. can cream of
    chicken soup
10-1/2 oz. can chicken broth
1/2 t. poultry seasoning
16-oz. can sliced carrots,
    drained

1-1/2 c. all-purpose flour
2 t. baking powder
1-1/2 c. buttermilk
1/2 c. butter, melted

Place chicken in a lightly greased 13"x9" baking pan. Combine soup,
broth and poultry seasoning in a mixing bowl; pour over chicken.
Arrange carrots on top; set aside. In a large bowl, mix together flour
and baking powder; add buttermilk and melted butter. Pour over
chicken mixture. Bake, uncovered, at 350 degrees for one hour, until
crust is golden. Serves 6.

Centerpieces that show off the red, white & blue couldn't
be easier. Simply fill jelly jars with red, white & blue
marbles, then tuck in mini pinwheels...so clever!

Turkey, Almond & Wild Rice Casserole

Shelley Turner
Boise, ID

*The crunch of almonds and the tang of pimentos
make this casserole oh-so delicious.*

1 onion, chopped
2 T. butter
1/2 c. all-purpose flour
2 4-1/2 oz. jars sliced
   mushrooms, drained and
   liquid reserved
3 c. half-and-half
1/2 to 1 c. chicken broth
6 c. cooked turkey, cubed

2 c. prepared long-grain
   wild rice
1 c. slivered almonds, toasted
1/2 c. pimentos, diced
4 T. fresh parsley, chopped
salt and pepper to taste
1 c. dry bread crumbs
1/4 c. butter, melted
Garnish: fresh parsley sprig

In a saucepan over medium heat, sauté onion in butter; remove from heat and stir in flour. Set aside. Combine reserved mushroom liquid with half-and-half and enough broth to make 4 cups. Gradually stir into flour mixture; cook and stir until thickened. Add turkey, rice, mushrooms, toasted almonds, pimentos, parsley, salt and pepper. Place in a lightly greased 11x17 baking pan; set aside. Combine bread crumbs and butter; sprinkle over top of casserole. Bake, uncovered, at 350 degrees for 40 minutes. Garnish, if desired. Serves 6 to 8.

Show your spirit when decorating for an Election Day Supper...toss red check fabric over tables and arrange white daisies in blue enamelware pails.

Quick Beefy Bean & Biscuit Bake

Hana Brosmer
Huntingburg, IN

Golden biscuits over a hearty filling make this meal satisfying.

1 lb. ground beef
1/2 c. onion, chopped
1 t. salt
1/2 t. pepper
28-oz. can brown sugar
   baked beans

1/4 c. barbecue sauce
1/4 c. catsup
1 c. shredded Cheddar cheese
16.3-oz. tube refrigerated
   buttermilk biscuits

Brown ground beef with onion, salt and pepper; drain. Add baked beans, barbecue sauce and catsup; pour into an ungreased 13"x9" baking pan. Sprinkle cheese evenly over top. Separate each biscuit into 2 equal thinner biscuits and arrange evenly on top. Bake, uncovered, at 350 degrees for 30 to 35 minutes, until bubbly and biscuits are golden. Makes 6 to 8 servings.

November days can be chilly...warm up with a mug of cider stirred with a cherry licorice twist!

Election Day Dinners

Mimi's Macaroni & Beef

Megan Thornton
Morristown, NJ

This dish was served by my mother and loved by everyone, from my college roommates to my own children. This super-easy recipe is best served immediately, but can be placed in a casserole dish and baked until heated through.

1 lb. ground beef
8-oz. can tomato sauce
16-oz. pkg. pasteurized process
    cheese spread, diced

16-oz. pkg. medium shell pasta,
    cooked

Brown beef over medium heat in a large pot; drain. Add sauce, cheese and pasta. Stir over low heat until cheese is melted. Serves 8 to 10.

There is always something for which to be thankful.
–Charles Dickens

Slow-Cooker Cola Ham

Elsie Mellinger
Annville, PA

*Baking a ham basted with cola produces
a delicious gravy...it's true!*

1/2 c. brown sugar, packed
1 t. dry mustard

12-oz. can cola
3 to 4-lb. fully-cooked ham

Combine brown sugar and mustard; add enough cola to make a glaze consistency and set aside. Place ham in a slow cooker; pour glaze over top, coating well. Cover and cook on low setting for 8 to 10 hours, basting occasionally with juices. Serves 8 to 10.

Ham is so versatile...friends can enjoy it as the
main dish, or sliced very thin and arranged on
split biscuits or bagels, it's an easy-to-eat sandwich.

Election Day Dinners

Cheesy New Potato Casserole

Dawn Van Horn
Columbia, NC

*Get ready to share this recipe when
you bring it to a church supper!*

10-oz. can diced tomatoes with
  green chiles
10-3/4 oz. can Cheddar
  cheese soup
10-3/4 oz. can cream of
  mushroom soup

3/4 c. water
1 T. dried, minced onion
salt and pepper to taste
10 to 12 new potatoes, peeled
  and thinly sliced
1/4 c. butter, diced

Combine tomatoes with chiles, soups, water, onion, salt and pepper in a large bowl; mix well to combine. Arrange potato slices in a lightly greased 13"x9" baking pan; pour tomato mixture over potatoes. Dot with butter. Bake, uncovered, at 350 degrees for one hour, until potatoes are tender when pierced with a fork. Serves 8.

When a recipe gives instructions to "dot with butter" try this quick & easy tip. Keep a stick of butter in the freezer, peel back the wrapper, then grate the butter directly over the baking pan...how easy!

Spanish Rice

Bobbi Crosson
Toledo, OH

When my 3 sons were little, they would want me to make this for our church potlucks...that way they knew there would be something there that they liked. My youngest son, now 35, called me for this recipe a couple of weeks ago.

1-1/2 lbs. ground beef
2 10-3/4 oz. cans tomato soup
1/4 c. green pepper, chopped

Optional: 1/4 c. onion, chopped
1-1/2 c. instant rice, cooked

Brown ground beef in a large skillet over medium heat; drain. Add tomato soup, green pepper and onion, if using; mix well. Add rice, stirring gently. Simmer for 15 minutes. Serves 8 to 10.

When deciding on a dish to share, keep in mind recipes made just for simmering all day in a slow cooker, or ones that are a snap to reheat in the oven or microwave.

Election Day Dinners

Casserole Onion Bread

Grace-Marie Hackwell
Gambier, OH

*Our family loves this bread right out of the oven...
it also makes great toast.*

1 c. milk
3 T. sugar
1-1/2 T. butter
3/4 c. water

1 env. active dry yeast
1-1/2 oz. pkg. onion soup mix
4 c. all-purpose flour

Heat milk in a saucepan over medium heat just until boiling. Pour into a medium bowl; add sugar and butter. Cool slightly. Heat water until very warm, about 110 to 115 degrees; add yeast and stir until dissolved. Add yeast mixture to milk mixture; add soup mix and flour. Stir to blend for 2 minutes. Cover bowl with a clean tea towel; let rise for 45 minutes, until double in bulk. Stir dough down; beat vigorously for 30 seconds. Turn into a greased 1-1/2 quart casserole dish. Bake, uncovered, at 375 degrees for 45 to 55 minutes. Tent with aluminum foil if top is browning too fast. Cool in pan on wire rack for 5 minutes; turn upside-down to remove. Serves 8 to 10.

If you're working the election, keep a mini cooler close by filled with quick snacks. Cheese cubes, apples, crackers, carrot and celery sticks, bottled water and juice boxes will all give you energy throughout the long day.

Slow-Cooker Pizza

Amanda Rickelman
Pulaski, IA

This is a great dish for any potluck gathering!

1/2 lb. ground beef
1 onion, chopped
8-oz. jar spaghetti sauce
16-oz. jar pizza sauce
12-oz. pkg. kluski egg noodles,
   cooked

8-oz. pkg. sliced pepperoni
8-oz. pkg. shredded mozzarella
   cheese
8-oz. pkg. shredded Cheddar
   cheese

Brown ground beef and onion in a large skillet over medium heat; drain. Stir in sauces; simmer until heated through. Layer half the noodles in a slow cooker and top with half each of meat sauce, pepperoni and cheeses. Repeat layering. Cover and cook on low setting for one hour, or on high setting for 30 minutes, until cheese is melted. Serves 8 to 10.

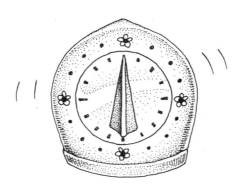

A slow cooker simmering away means at the day's end,
you can enjoy a hearty, homestyle meal with
practically no effort at all...what a time saver!

Election Day Dinners

Paula's Baked Ziti

Theresa Reynolds
Groton, CT

This is our most requested dish at every potluck...
it's super simple to make too.

1 lb. ground beef, browned
    and drained
4 c. ziti pasta, cooked
28-oz. jar spaghetti sauce

1 c. grated Parmesan-Romano
    cheese, divided
8-oz. pkg. shredded mozzarella
    cheese

Combine beef, ziti, sauce and 3/4 cup grated cheese in a large bowl; mix well. Spread in a lightly greased 13"x9" baking pan; sprinkle with mozzarella cheese. Bake, uncovered, at 375 degrees for about 20 minutes, until hot and bubbly. Garnish with remaining grated cheese. Serves 6.

A roomy picnic basket makes light work of toting plates, silverware, napkins and cups to any potluck or carry-in.

Cheesy Chicken Fettuccine

Margaret Scoresby
Mosinee, WI

*We have served this to the basketball team when
they come over for dinner and also take it to
church potlucks and family get-togethers.*

10-3/4 oz. can cream of
   mushroom soup
8-oz. pkg. cream cheese, cubed
4-oz. can sliced mushrooms,
   drained
1 c. whipping cream
1/2 c. butter, softened
1/4 t. garlic powder

3/4 c. grated Parmesan cheese
1/2 c. shredded mozzarella
   cheese
1/2 c. shredded Swiss cheese
2-1/2 c. cooked chicken, cubed
8-oz. pkg. fettuccine pasta,
   cooked

Combine soup, cream cheese, mushrooms, cream, butter and garlic
powder in a large pot over medium heat. Stir in cheeses until melted.
Add chicken; heat through. Stir in fettuccine. Spread in a lightly
greased 2-quart casserole dish; sprinkle with topping. Cover and bake
at 350 degrees for 25 minutes. Uncover and bake for an additional
5 to 10 minutes, until golden. Serves 8.

Topping:

1/3 c. seasoned dry bread
   crumbs
2 T. butter, melted

1 to 2 T. grated Parmesan
   cheese

Combine all ingredients in a small bowl.

Who says ice cream cones can only hold ice cream? Fill cones
with red, white & blue fruit salad...simply toss together whole
blueberries, sliced strawberries and mini marshmallows!

Chicken Noodle Casserole

Wanda Freeman
Krum, TX

This is a family favorite casserole...warm and comforting.
It's easy to make ahead and travels great. You can also
make this ahead of time and freeze it to enjoy later.

1/4 c. butter
1 onion, chopped
1 green pepper, chopped
5 to 6 stalks celery, chopped
4-oz. jar diced pimentos,
    drained
4-oz. can diced green chiles
10-3/4 oz. can cream of
    mushroom soup

3 9-3/4 oz. cans chicken,
    drained slightly
12-oz. pkg. elbow macaroni,
    cooked
12-oz. pkg. shredded Mexican-
    blend cheese, divided

Melt butter in a Dutch oven over medium heat. Add onion, green
pepper, celery, pimentos and chiles; sauté until tender. Stir in soup and
chicken with liquid. Simmer for 10 minutes. Spread macaroni in a
lightly greased 13"x9" baking pan; sprinkle with half the cheese.
Spread chicken mixture over cheese; stir gently. Sprinkle with
remaining cheese. Bake, uncovered, at 350 degrees for 30 minutes,
until cheese is bubbly and golden. Let stand for 5 minutes before
serving. Serves 12.

Whip up a side dish in no time at all...layer thick slices
of juicy tomatoes with fresh mozzarella cheese,
then drizzle with olive oil.

Angel Biscuits

Cheryl Donnelly
Arvada, CO

I remember my mom making these biscuits when I was little...
they always made our home smell so good. My mom still
makes them, and now so do I for my own family.

5 c. all-purpose flour
1 t. baking soda
1 T. baking powder
1 t. salt
3 T. sugar

3/4 c. shortening
1/4 c. water
1 env. active dry yeast
1-3/4 c. buttermilk

Combine flour, baking soda, baking powder, salt and sugar in a large bowl; mix well. Cut in shortening until crumbly. Heat water until warm, about 110 to 115 degrees. Stir in yeast; let dissolve. Stir in buttermilk. Add mixture to flour mixture until all flour is moistened. Cover bowl; refrigerate overnight. Roll dough out on a lightly floured surface to 1/2-inch thick. Cut into circles using a 2-1/2" round cookie cutter; arrange on ungreased baking sheets. Bake at 400 degrees for 12 to 15 minutes, until golden. Makes one dozen.

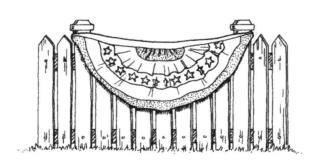

Keep an eye open for sales after the Fourth of July...
you'll find oodles of patriotic cups, napkins, plates,
banners, buntings and flags to use for spirited
decorating when Election Day rolls around.

Election Day Dinners

Lighter-Than-Air Potato Rolls

Linda Cuellar
Riverside, CA

*These are wonderful right out of the oven served
with butter, jam, apple butter or honey.*

1/2 c. instant potato flakes	1/2 c. hot water
1 t. sugar	1/3 c. cold water
2 T. butter, softened	2 c. biscuit baking mix

Stir together potato flakes, sugar, butter and hot water. Stir in cold
water and baking mix. Gently smooth dough into a ball on a floured
surface; knead 8 to 10 times. Roll out into a 10"x6" rectangle. Cut
into 12 squares; arrange on an ungreased baking sheet. Bake at
450 degrees for about 10 minutes. Makes one dozen.

Bring along the sweetest pats of butter to serve with
Lighter-Than-Air Potato Rolls. Butter slices cut with
mini cookie cutters or pressed with cookie stamps
make it easy to be creative.

Susan's Fork-Tender Roast

Susan Dillard
Oldtown, ID

The gravy with this roast is delicious. Add some chopped carrots and celery with the onion, if you like.

1 onion, chopped
3 to 4-lb. beef chuck roast
1-oz. pkg. ranch salad
  dressing mix

1-oz. pkg. Italian salad
  dressing mix
.87-oz. pkg. brown gravy mix
1/2 c. water

Place onion in the bottom of a slow cooker; set aside. Combine mixes and rub half of mixture over roast; place roast in slow cooker. Sprinkle on remaining mixture and pour water around roast. Cover and cook on low setting for 7 to 9 hours. Serves 6 to 8.

If your Election Day Supper is a community event, be sure to post signs and advertise in the local paper so no one misses all the fun and good food!

Fruit Salsa with Cinnamon Chips, page 49

Spinach & Bacon Quiche, page 40

Southern-Style Breakfast Casserole, page 8

Make-Ahead Ham & Cheese Casserole, page 14

Strawberry Fruit Dip, page 54

Easy Southern-Style Pork Barbecue, page 62

Mommy's Antipasto Salad, page 65

Frosted Banana Bars, page 202

Grandma's Baked Mac & Cheese, page 178

Heavenly Deviled Eggs, page 60

Chicken & Asparagus Bake, page 46

Church Supper Tuna Bake, page 172

South-of-the-Border Chicken Soup, page 38

Barb's Easy Lasagna, page 128

Everyone's Favorite Vegetable Soup, page 149

Peanut Butter Texas Sheet Cake, page 186

Caramel Fudge Brownies, page 212

Famous Calico Beans, page 67

Just Perfect Sloppy Joes, page 56

Turkey, Almond & Wild Rice Casserole, page 111

Mandarin Orange Salad, page 183

Pasta Bake Florentine, page 43

Tennessee Fudge Pie, page 199

Pronto Pasta Skillet

Kathy Epperly
Wichita, KS

*I like to whip this up right after church since it's both quick
& easy. You can cook the pasta and chop the veggies
ahead of time to make it even quicker.*

1 lb. boneless beef sirloin steak,
   sliced thinly into strips
1/4 c. balsamic vinaigrette,
   divided
14-1/2 oz. can stewed tomatoes
1 onion, sliced

1 green pepper, chopped
8-oz. can sliced mushrooms,
   drained
1/2 c. pasteurized process
   cheese sauce
16-oz. pkg. penne pasta, cooked

In a large skillet over medium-high heat, brown steak in 2 tablespoons
vinaigrette for 2 minutes, until browned on all sides. Stir in tomatoes
with juice, onion, green pepper, mushrooms and remaining vinaigrette.
Bring to a boil; reduce heat to medium and simmer for 10 minutes,
until onion and pepper are crisp-tender. Remove from heat. Spoon
cheese sauce over top. Let stand for 2 to 3 minutes, until cheese is
melted. Serve over prepared pasta. Serves 4.

It's a good idea to keep aluminum foil, plastic zipping bags
and plastic wrap on hand for wrapping up leftovers, or for
someone who may just want to take a sampler plate home!

Stew with Gravy for Jill

Maureen Perlette
Fuquay Varina, NC

As I would tuck my daughter Jill in for bedtime, she would always want to know what we were having for dinner the next night. She told me years later that it made her go to sleep happy if we were having a dinner with gravy. The memories and friendship she gave me will last a lifetime...I dedicate this recipe to Jill, my sweetie.

1/3 c. instant pearl tapioca,
   uncooked
1/2 t. dried basil
2 T. sugar
1/2 t. pepper
46-oz. can tomato juice

2 onions, quartered
4 carrots, peeled and cut into
   3-inch pieces
3 stalks celery, chopped
2 lbs. stew beef, cubed
cooked egg noodles

Combine tapioca, basil, sugar and pepper in a slow cooker; add tomato juice, mixing well. Add vegetables and stew beef. Cover and cook on low setting for 10 to 12 hours. Serve over egg noodles. Serves 6.

Resist the temptation to lift the lid on a slow cooker...
it can take as long as 20 minutes for it to regain
the heat lost when the lid is removed.

Cheddar & Green Pepper Cornbread

Darlene Fuller
Greenville, KY

One of our favorite comfort foods is cornbread and this variation is our favorite!

1 c. self-rising flour
1 c. cornmeal
1 egg, beaten
1-1/2 c. milk
1 c. corn
1/2 c. green pepper, chopped
1 c. shredded Cheddar cheese
1/4 t. onion salt

Combine flour, cornmeal, egg and milk until moistened. Stir in remaining ingredients; mix well. Spread in a lightly greased 13"x9" baking pan. Bake at 375 degrees for 30 minutes, until golden. Serves 10 to 12.

Whip up a crock of Honey Bee Butter to serve with warm cornbread or rolls. Simply combine one cup honey with one cup softened butter and one teaspoon vanilla extract.

Heavenly Onion Casserole

Lynne Bishop
Antioch, TN

This was handed down to me from my mother who would always take it to our church dinners. The pastor would ask her to bring this special, flavorful dish. He liked the name she gave it, for it truly was heavenly!

3 T. butter
3 onions, sliced
8-oz. pkg. sliced mushrooms
1 c. shredded Swiss cheese
10-3/4 oz. can cream of
    mushroom soup

1 c. evaporated milk
2 t. soy sauce
6 to 8 slices French bread
6 to 8 slices deli Swiss cheese

Melt butter in a large skillet over medium heat. Add onions and mushrooms; cook until tender. Spread in a lightly greased 11"x7" baking pan; sprinkle with shredded cheese. Combine soup, milk and soy sauce; pour over cheese. Top with bread slices, then cheese slices. Cover and refrigerate for 4 hours, or overnight. Bake, loosely covered, at 375 degrees for 30 minutes. Uncover and bake for an additional 15 to 20 minutes, until heated through. Let stand for 5 minutes before serving. Serves 6 to 8.

Icy lemonade and frosty juices are sure thirst quenchers. To keep beverages from watering down, freeze juice in ice cube trays and use in place of ordinary ice. Just for fun, freeze a cherry or a lemon slice with the juice.

Slow-Cooker Chicken with Rice

Vickie
Gooseberry Patch

Slow cooking keeps the chicken oh-so tender and moist.

4 boneless, skinless
  chicken breasts
1/4 t. salt
1/4 t. pepper
1/4 t. paprika
1 T. oil
14-1/2 oz. can crushed
  tomatoes

1 red pepper, chopped
1 onion, chopped
1 clove garlic, minced
1/2 t. dried rosemary
10-oz. pkg. frozen peas
cooked rice

Sprinkle chicken with seasonings; set aside. Heat oil in a medium skillet over medium-high heat; add chicken and cook until golden on all sides. Arrange chicken in a slow cooker. In a small bowl, combine remaining ingredients except peas and rice; pour over chicken. Cover and cook on low setting for 7 to 9 hours, or on high setting for 3 to 4 hours. One hour before serving, stir in peas. Serve over rice. Makes 4 servings.

Don't worry about transferring slow-cooker meals into serving dishes…they'll stay nice and warm served right from the slow cooker. And if you set a table tent alongside your slow cooker, everyone will know just what's inside.

Coconut Cream Cake

Sharon Tillman
Hampton, VA

Smooth & creamy...you won't go home with a single slice!

18-1/2 oz. pkg. white cake mix
   with pudding
3 eggs
1/3 c. oil
1 c. water
1/2 t. coconut extract

14-oz. can sweetened
   condensed milk
15-oz. can cream of coconut
1 c. heavy whipping cream
1 T. white sugar
1 c. sweetened, flaked coconut

Mix together cake mix, eggs, oil, water and coconut extract; beat for 2 minutes. Pour into a greased and floured 13"x9" baking pan. Bake at 350 degrees for 30 minutes, or until a toothpick inserted near center of cake tests clean. Combine condensed milk and cream of coconut; stir until smooth. With a large fork, poke holes in even rows all over cake; pour milk mixture over top. Refrigerate for several hours or overnight. In a large bowl, beat cream until soft peaks form. Add sugar; beat until stiff. Spread over cooled cake; sprinkle with coconut. Serves 24.

Desserts are so
tempting, you may
want to offer a sampler
plate for those who
just can't decide!

Granny's Shoo Fly Pie

Kristi Boyle
Easton, MD

*My children love it when we go to Granny's house
and she has just pulled a shoo fly pie out of the oven!*

1 t. baking soda
1 c. hot water
1/2 c. brown sugar, packed

3 eggs, beaten
1 c. molasses
9-inch pie crust

Dissolve baking soda in hot water in a mixing bowl. Add remaining ingredients except pie crust. Pour half the mixture into pie crust; sprinkle with 3/4 cup crumb topping. Pour remaining molasses mixture over crumbs; sprinkle with remaining crumb topping. Bake at 400 degrees for 10 minutes. Reduce heat to 375 degrees and bake for an additional 50 minutes. Serves 8.

Crumb Topping:

2-1/2 c. all-purpose flour
1 c. brown sugar, packed

1/2 c. shortening

Combine flour and brown sugar; mix well. Cut in shortening until crumbly.

Set up a table with slow cookers of chocolatey cocoa or warm spiced cider...a welcome way to warm up on a chilly autumn night.

Supreme Vanilla Delight

Linda Molloy
Syracuse, NY

This is an adaption of one of my favorite chocolate recipes...
my grandkids love it!

18-1/2 oz. pkg. white cake mix
3.4-oz. pkg. instant vanilla
   pudding mix
3 eggs, beaten
1 c. oil

1 c. water
6-oz. pkg. white chocolate chips
Garnish: ice cream or whipped
   cream

Mix together all ingredients except garnish and pour into a greased slow cooker. Cover and cook on high setting for 5 hours. Serve topped with ice cream or whipped cream. Serves 8 to 12.

Make each day a little better than the one before.
–Gordon B. Hinckley

Texas 2-Step Apple Crisp

Jennifer Swartz
Smithville, TX

So tasty, no need to dress it up, but a dollop of whipped cream dusted with cinnamon is a scrumptious topper!

6 cooking apples, peeled, cored
   and sliced
1-1/2 c. all-purpose flour
1 c. brown sugar, packed
1 T. cinnamon
1/2 t. nutmeg

1/4 t. ground ginger
3/4 c. butter, softened
Garnish: vanilla ice cream,
   whipped topping,
   maraschino cherries

Arrange apple slices in a greased slow cooker; set aside. Combine remaining ingredients except garnish in a bowl. Mix well and sprinkle over apples, pressing down lightly. Cover and cook on high setting for 4 hours, until apples are tender. Garnish as desired. Makes 6 to 8 servings.

Slip a water-filled Mason jar of white daisies or mums inside
a pair of red cowboy boots and set them by the door...
you can even tuck in a mini flag. Now that's a clever,
patriotic welcome Texas-style!

Old-Fashioned Chocolate Pie

Corinna King
Mars Hill, NC

*This is by far my husband's favorite pie. It's ooey-gooey
and tastes like both fudge and brownies.*

6 T. butter
1/4 c. baking cocoa
1 c. sugar
2 eggs

1/4 c. evaporated milk
1 t. vanilla extract
9-inch pie crust

Melt butter in a saucepan over medium heat; add cocoa and sugar,
stirring well. Remove from heat; add eggs, one at a time, mixing well
after each addition. Stir in milk and vanilla, blending well; pour
into pie crust. Bake at 400 degrees for 5 minutes. Reduce heat to
325 degrees and bake for an additional 30 to 35 minutes. Serves 8.

Dip maraschino cherries in melted chocolate for
an out-of-this-world pie or cake garnish.

Grandma Eichberger's Cheesecake

Lori Johnson
Lincoln, NE

My grandmother had 5 boys and 27 grandchildren.
All of her desserts were wonderful, but this one is the best!

8-oz. pkg. cream cheese,
   softened
8-oz. container frozen whipped
   topping, thawed

1 c. powdered sugar
9-inch graham cracker crust
21-oz. can cherry pie filling

Blend together cream cheese, whipped topping and powdered sugar in
a bowl; mix well. Spread in crust; chill for 2 hours. Spread pie filling
over top. Serves 6 to 8.

For easier mixing, allow cheesecake ingredients to
stand at room temperature for at least 30 minutes.

Sweet Potato Pie

Irene Robinson
Cincinnati, OH

We like this served with a big scoop of ice cream.

14-1/2 oz. can sweet potatoes,
    drained and mashed
3/4 c. milk
3/4 c. brown sugar, packed
2 eggs, beaten

1 T. butter, melted
1/2 t. salt
1/2 t. cinnamon
9-inch pie crust

Combine all ingredients except crust in a blender; process until smooth. Pour into pie crust. Bake at 400 degrees for 10 minutes. Cover edges of crust with aluminum foil. Reduce heat to 350 degrees; bake for an additional 35 minutes, until a knife tip inserted in center comes out clean. Serves 6 to 8.

Serve pudding, cake or brownies layered between scoops
of ice cream in an old-fashioned sundae cup
or banana split bowl. How fun!

Soup Suppers & Chili Cook-offs

Kathi's Chili

1-1/2 lbs. ground
   beef sirloin
1 yellow onion, diced
15-1/2 oz. can dark
   red kidney beans,
   drained and rinsed
15-1/2 oz. can light
   red kidney beans,
   drained and rinsed

28-oz. can diced
   tomatoes
1-1/4 oz. pkg. mild
   chili seasoning mix
1-1/4 oz. pkg. hot
   chili seasoning mix

Brown ground beef in a Dutch oven; drain.
Add onion and green pepper; saute until
vegetables are tender. Stir in beans,
tomatoes and seasoning mixes. Simmer over
medium heat for 10 minutes. Makes 6 servings.

1st

Carrie's Gone-in-a-Flash Chili

Carrie Lassiter
Rancho Cucamonga, CA

I entered this chili in our church's Chili Cook-Off and it was gone before the judging began! If I want it a bit thicker, I just add a can of refried beans.

1 lb. ground beef
1 onion, diced
1 clove garlic, minced
2 to 3 t. chili powder
14-oz. can kidney beans, drained and rinsed

14-oz. can pinto beans, drained and rinsed
14-oz. can stewed tomatoes
15-oz. can tomato sauce
16-oz. jar salsa
3 T. Worcestershire sauce

Brown ground beef in a large Dutch oven over medium heat. Add onion, garlic and chili powder. Cook until onion is translucent and chili powder is fragrant; drain. Add remaining ingredients; mix thoroughly. Bring to a boil. Reduce heat; simmer for 20 to 30 minutes, or until heated through. Makes 6 servings.

Serve up chili topped with homemade croutons...so good!
Use cookie cutters to cut out fun shapes from slices of bread,
then brush cut-outs with butter and a sprinkling of herbs.
Bake in a 200-degree oven until croutons are golden.

Creamy White Chicken Chili

Mary Van Peursem
Kasson, MN

This was a winner at one of our church potlucks.

1 lb. boneless, skinless chicken,
    cubed
1 onion, chopped
1-1/2 t. garlic powder
1 T. oil
2 15-1/2 oz. cans Great
    Northern beans, drained
    and rinsed
14-1/2 oz. can chicken broth

2 4-oz. cans green chiles
1 t. salt
1 t. ground cumin
1 t. dried oregano
1/2 t. pepper
1/4 t. cayenne pepper
8-oz. container sour cream
1/2 c. whipping cream

In a large saucepan over medium heat, sauté chicken, onion and garlic powder in oil until no longer pink. Add beans, broth, chiles and seasonings; bring to a boil. Reduce heat; simmer, uncovered, for 30 minutes. Remove from heat; stir in sour cream and whipping cream. Serve immediately. Makes 8 servings.

Plan a chili cook-off for early February...the snow is still piling up outside, making it the perfect time for a warm-you-to-your-toes bowl of chili! Invite everyone to stir up a pot of their favorite chili, then have a friendly judging of whose is the tastiest. You can even hand out wooden spoons, oven mitts and aprons as prizes!

Cincinnati-Style Chili

Jennifer Oglesby
Brownsville, IN

*Living right on the border of Ohio, we've come to love
Cincinnati-style chili. This is my husband's most
requested recipe, and a definite family favorite.*

2 lbs. ground beef
4 c. water
8-oz. can tomato sauce
1 T. Worcestershire sauce
1 t. vinegar
1 onion, finely chopped
1 t. garlic, minced
3 T. chili powder
3 T. ground cumin

2 T. allspice
2 bay leaves
1 t. cinnamon
1 t. nutmeg
1 t. celery seed
1 t. salt
cooked spaghetti
Garnish: grated Cheddar cheese

Combine uncooked ground beef and water in a large pot. Add
remaining ingredients except spaghetti and cheese. Simmer over
medium heat for 3 hours, stirring often. Discard bay leaves. Serve
over spaghetti and top with cheese. Serves 6.

Other things may change us, but we start and end with family.
–Anthony Brandt

Cheesy Sesame Seed Muffins

Irene Robinson
Cincinnati, OH

These easy, tasty muffins are golden and pillowy.

2 T. butter, divided
1/2 c. onion, chopped
1-1/2 c. biscuit baking mix
1 c. sharp American cheese,
    shredded and divided

1 egg, beaten
1/2 c. milk
1 T. sesame seed, toasted

Melt one tablespoon butter in a skillet over medium heat. Add onion; stir constantly until tender, about 3 minutes. Combine onion, baking mix and 1/2 cup cheese in a large bowl. In a separate bowl, combine egg and milk; add to onion mixture, stirring just until moistened. Spoon batter into lightly greased muffin cups, filling 1/2 full. Sprinkle with remaining cheese and sesame seed; dot with remaining butter. Bake at 400 degrees for 13 minutes, or until golden. Remove from pan immediately and serve warm. Makes one dozen.

Cornbread and chili are made for each other! Shake up your best cornbread recipe by adding some shredded Cheddar cheese, crisply cooked and crumbled bacon, diced green chiles or a drained can of corn.

Nana's Potato Soup

Christy Bonner
Berry, AL

*Handed down in my family for many generations, this
recipe can always be found at our winter church
socials. It's true comfort food for a chilly evening.*

1/2 c. margarine
10 T. all-purpose flour
4 14-1/2 oz. cans chicken
   broth
1 T. fresh chives, chopped
1 T. fresh parsley, chopped
4 c. half-and-half

6 to 8 potatoes, peeled, cubed
   and cooked
salt and pepper to taste
Garnish: shredded Cheddar
   cheese, bacon bits,
   chopped green onions

Melt margarine in a Dutch oven over medium heat. Stir in flour one
tablespoon at a time until smooth. Add broth, chives and parsley;
stir until thickened. Add half-and-half, stirring until well mixed. Stir
in potatoes and heat through; sprinkle to taste with salt and pepper.
Garnish as desired. Makes 6 to 8 servings.

A soup supper is a wonderful way to spend a crisp autumn
afternoon with friends. Ask them to bring a slow cooker of
their favorite soup, and you'll supply the rolls, butter, beverages,
bowls and spoons...then settle in and enjoy time
catching up with one another.

Tuscan Soup

Rhoda Rine
Mount Vernon, OH

This is one of our favorite soups to enjoy
after our Sunday meetings.

1 lb. ground pork sausage
3/4 c. onion, diced
1 slice bacon, diced
1-1/4 t. garlic, minced
2 T. chicken bouillon granules
4 c. water
2 potatoes, halved lengthwise
  and cut into 1/4-inch strips
2 c. kale, thinly sliced
3/4 c. whipping cream

Brown sausage in a large pot over medium heat; drain and set aside. Add onion and bacon to pot; cook over medium heat until onion is almost translucent. Add garlic; cook for one minute. Add bouillon, water and potatoes; simmer for 15 minutes, until potatoes are tender. Stir in kale, sausage and whipping cream; heat through over low heat without boiling. Serves 6 to 8.

A crispy salad or chilled fruit is so nice served alongside a bowl of steaming soup. Just for fun, spoon salad or fruit into hollowed-out tomato halves, or line berry pails with leaf lettuce and then spoon inside. So pretty on a buffet table!

Slow-Cooker Taco Soup

Susan Ahlstrand
Post Falls, ID

A friend from my Bible study group made her version of this and everyone loved it! I changed a few ingredients to suit my tastes.

1 lb. ground beef
1 onion, diced
1 clove garlic, minced
12-oz. bottle green taco sauce
4-oz. can green chiles
2 to 3   15-oz. cans black beans,
    drained and rinsed

15-1/4 oz. can corn, drained
15-oz. can tomato sauce
2 c. water
1-1/4 oz. pkg. taco seasoning
    mix
Garnish: sour cream, shredded
    Cheddar cheese, corn chips

Brown beef, onion and garlic in a large skillet over medium heat; drain. In a slow cooker, combine beef mixture and remaining ingredients except garnish. Cover and cook on high setting for one hour. Serve with sour cream, shredded cheese and corn chips. Serves 8 to 10.

Even garnishes can be dressed up. When you're sharing a pot
of Slow-Cooker Taco Soup, line a new terra cotta pot with
wax paper and shredded cheese, or add corn chips
to a bandanna-lined sombrero...what fun!

Everyone's Favorite Vegetable Soup

Marcel Beers
Easton, PA

This was always my favorite soup,
now it's my one-year-old's favorite too.

1 lb. stew beef, cubed
1 T. oil
4 potatoes, peeled and diced
16-oz. pkg. frozen peas
16-oz. pkg. frozen corn

16-oz. pkg. baby carrots
2 12-oz. jars beef gravy
2 15-oz. cans tomato sauce
salt and pepper to taste

Brown beef in oil in a large skillet over medium heat; drain. Add potatoes; cook until softened. Combine beef mixture and remaining ingredients in a slow cooker. Cover and cook on low setting for 8 hours, or until carrots and potatoes are tender, stirring occasionally. Makes 8 servings.

Tag sales and flea markets are the best places to find roomy serving bowls, oversize pots & pans and oodles of flatware...all finds that will come in extra-handy for your next get-together.

Broccoli-Cheese Cornbread

Jane Reynolds
Rowlett, TX

This recipe, given to me by my Aunt Ora Lee, is one I enjoy toting to potluck dinners at church and at work.

1/2 c. margarine, softened
10-oz. pkg. frozen chopped
   broccoli, thawed
1-1/2 c. cottage cheese
1 onion, chopped

5 eggs, beaten
2 8-1/2 oz. pkgs. cornbread
   mix
1 c. shredded Cheddar cheese

Mix together all ingredients except cheese; spread in a lightly greased 13"x9" baking pan. Bake, uncovered, at 325 degrees for 45 minutes. Sprinkle with cheese and bake for an additional 3 minutes, until cheese is melted. Makes about 12 servings.

When serving pitchers of ice water or lemonade,
rub a bit of wax paper along the rim of the pitcher...
no more drips while pouring!

House of Bowles Chili

Shirley Bowles
Wyoming, DE

I worked the night shift in a large nursing home for 16 years, and whenever it was my turn to bring the entrée for a potluck, I always brought this chili. The first night I brought it in, someone had written the recipe down, and then left a copy on my desk so I would always make it the same!

1 T. oil
1 green pepper, chopped
1 onion, chopped
2 lbs. ground beef, chicken
    or turkey
2 1-1/4 oz. pkgs. chili
    seasoning mix

2 14-oz. cans stewed tomatoes,
    crushed
12-oz. can tomato paste
2 15-oz. cans kidney beans,
    drained and rinsed

Heat oil in a large skillet over medium heat; sauté pepper and onion until tender. Add ground meat. Cook until browned; drain. Add remaining ingredients, stirring well; pour into a slow cooker. Cover and cook on low setting for 6 to 8 hours. Makes 6 to 8 servings.

Have friends, not for the sake of receiving, but of giving.
–Joseph Roux

Homestyle Tomato-Basil Soup

Gretchen Ham
Pine City, NY

This soup is always the one asked for when we have our Sunday soup & sandwich lunches after church services.

1/2 c. butter
1 c. fresh basil, chopped
2 28-oz. cans crushed
    tomatoes
2 cloves garlic, minced

4 c. half-and-half
salt and pepper to taste
Garnish: croutons, grated
    Parmesan cheese

Melt butter over medium heat in a large saucepan. Add basil; sauté for 2 minutes. Add tomatoes and garlic; simmer for an additional 20 minutes. Remove from heat; let stand until just warm. Transfer mixture to a blender and purée in batches. Strain into a clean pan; add half-and-half, mixing very well. Reheat soup over medium-low heat. Garnish with croutons and sprinkle with Parmesan cheese. Makes 10 servings.

Sometimes it's hard for little ones to wait while dinner's being served. Have crayons, stickers and paper on hand so they can create their own special placemats.

Pastina Soup

Althea Paquette
South Attleboro, MA

This recipe is from my Italian grandmother,
who always served it with warm slices of Italian bread.
The easiest soup to make, and I think, the best!

1 meaty beef shank bone
6 carrots, peeled and sliced
6 stalks celery, diced
2 onions, chopped
3 tomatoes, diced

salt and pepper to taste
16-oz. pkg. orzo pasta,
  uncooked
Garnish: grated Parmesan
  cheese

Cover beef shank with water in a soup pot; bring to a boil over
medium heat. Add carrots, celery, onions, tomatoes, salt and pepper.
Simmer over low heat for 6 to 8 hours. Remove beef shank, returning
beef to soup pot; discard bone. In a separate pan, cook orzo for
4 minutes; drain and add to soup. Simmer for an additional 5 minutes.
Sprinkle with Parmesan cheese. Serves 8.

Plastic straws, rolled napkins and flatware are easy for everyone
to reach when you place them in children's sand pails,
new terra cotta pots, Mason jars or berry baskets.

Friendship Christmas Soup

Diana Krol
Nickerson, KS

This soup was served for many years at the Nickerson Methodist Church's Christmas auction. The women from the church would each bring an ingredient and the soup would simmer all afternoon before the annual auction. It was always served with homemade French bread and a variety of pies...yum!

3 T. oil
1 meaty beef soup bone
1 onion, chopped
1/2 t. turmeric
1-1/2 t. salt
1/8 t. pepper
1 bay leaf
1/8 t. dried thyme

1/8 t. allspice
1/8 t. dried sage
1-1/2 qts. water
1 qt. tomato juice
1 c. carrots, peeled and chopped
1 c. celery, chopped
1 head cabbage, shredded
16-oz. can green beans

Heat oil in a large soup pot over medium heat. Brown soup bone and onion; remove soup bone and set aside. Add just enough turmeric to turn onion yellow. Stir in remaining seasonings; cook for 3 to 5 minutes. Add water, tomato juice, carrots, celery, cabbage, green beans with liquid and soup bone. Simmer, covered, for 3 to 5 hours. Remove soup bone; cut meat off bone and return meat to soup. Skim fat from surface; discard bay leaf. Serve hot. Makes 8 to 12 servings.

Clever invitations...jot down all the details on recipe cards, punch a hole in the corner of each and use jute to tie cards to the handles of wooden spoons.

Kathi's Chili

Kathi Gormley
Chicago, IL

After my mom passed away many years ago, I wanted to make her chili recipe for my dad and grandfather...only her recipe was never written down! After trying to find the perfect mix of beef, beans, tomatoes and seasonings, I created a combination that we feel tastes a lot like my mom's.

1-1/2 lbs. ground beef sirloin
1 yellow onion, diced
1/2 c. green pepper, diced
15-1/2 oz. can dark red kidney
    beans, drained and rinsed
15-1/2 oz. can light red kidney
    beans, drained and rinsed

28-oz. can diced tomatoes
1-1/4-oz. pkg. mild chili
    seasoning mix
1-1/4 oz. pkg. hot chili
    seasoning mix

Brown ground beef in a Dutch oven; drain. Add onion and green pepper; sauté until vegetables are tender. Stir in beans, tomatoes and seasoning mixes. Simmer over medium heat for 10 minutes. Makes 6 servings.

If you've added a bit too much hot chili seasoning, it's easy to cool it off...simply stir a tablespoon each of lemon or lime juice and sugar into the chili.

Italian Sausage Soup

Alicia VanDuyne
Braidwood, IL

Truly, a stick-to-your-ribs soup...hearty, filling and delicious.

1 onion, chopped
3 carrots, peeled and chopped
4 stalks celery, chopped
1 T. garlic, chopped
4 10-1/2 oz. cans beef broth
1 T. Italian seasoning
1 lb. Italian pork link sausage,
  cooked, drained and sliced

6-oz. can tomato paste
10-oz. pkg. frozen chopped
  spinach, thawed and drained
8-oz. pkg. frozen cheese
  tortellini

Combine onion, carrots, celery, garlic, beef broth and Italian seasoning
in a large stockpot; bring to a boil over medium heat. Reduce heat;
simmer for 10 minutes. Add sausage, tomato paste and spinach; heat
through, about 5 minutes. Stir in tortellini; cook until tender, about
15 to 20 minutes. Serves 6 to 8.

Offer individual servings of savory fall soups spooned
into pint-size hollowed-out Jack-be-Little pumpkins.

Garlicky Green Chili

Tammy Burnett
Springfield, MO

My boss gave me this recipe, and I've found that every time
I prepare it, guests ask me for the recipe!

3 lbs. boneless pork chops,
   cubed
2 T. oil
1/4 c. all-purpose flour
2 T. garlic, minced
salt and pepper to taste

2 4-oz. cans diced green chiles
14-1/2 oz. can chicken broth
16-oz. jar chunky salsa
1 bunch fresh cilantro, chopped
1 t. ground cumin

In a Dutch oven over medium heat, brown pork in oil. Mix in flour;
stir for one minute. Add garlic, salt and pepper, cook for 2 minutes.
Stir in remaining ingredients; simmer for 45 minutes. Serves 8.

Sometimes a chili cook-off is held with only the men
whipping up their favorite batch of chili...they get
bragging rights to their secret recipes, and the ladies
get a night off from cooking!

Kielbasa & Veggie Soup

Karen Puchnick
Butler, PA

This soup is a creation of mine after enjoying a Kielbasa soup at a local restaurant many moons ago...perfect on a chilly day.

2 T. butter
1-lb. pkg. Kielbasa, diced
1 onion, chopped
1 c. celery, peeled and chopped
5 c. water
2 c. carrots, sliced
4 to 5 c. beef broth
10-3/4 oz. can tomato soup

2 to 3 T. catsup
2 T. vinegar
1 bay leaf
1/2 t. dried thyme
1 T. salt
3/4 t. pepper
2 c. potatoes, peeled and cubed

Heat butter in a large soup kettle over medium heat. Add Kielbasa, onion and celery; cook, stirring occasionally, until vegetables are tender. Add water and remaining ingredients except potatoes. Simmer, covered, over low heat for one hour. Add potatoes and cook for an additional hour. Discard bay leaf. Serves 8 to 10.

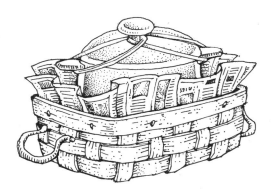

Keep a stockpot or slow-cooker lid where it belongs!
Wrap a long, heavy-duty rubber band around a pot handle,
twist it, and wrap over the lid and around the knob,
then secure it to the handle on the other side.

Savory Chicken Soup

Estella Hickman
Gooseberry Patch

Oh, how the aroma of this simmering soup fills the kitchen.

2 carrots, peeled and sliced
2 stalks celery, chopped
2 to 3 potatoes, peeled and
  quartered
Optional: 2 onions, sliced
3 boneless, skinless chicken
  breasts, cubed

14-1/2 oz. can chicken broth
2 c. water
1/4 t. salt
1/4 t. pepper
1/2 t. dried parsley
1/2 t. dried basil

Place all vegetables in a slow cooker; add chicken. Pour in broth and water; sprinkle seasonings over top. Cover and cook on low setting for 8 hours, or on high setting for 4 hours. Serves 4 to 6.

In my grandmother's house there was always chicken soup
And talk of the old country...
–Louis Simpson

Ivan's Chili

Angie Whitmore
Farmington, UT

I got this recipe almost 20 years ago from a co-worker who named it after her husband. I make this every winter after the first snowfall and serve it with homemade cornbread.

3 c. dried red beans
28-oz. can peeled tomatoes,
   chopped
3 8-oz. cans tomato sauce
3 T. chili powder
1 t. dried oregano
1/2 t. sugar
1 t. salt

1 t. garlic salt
3/4 t. pepper
1 onion, diced
1 to 2 cloves garlic, diced
1 T. oil
1 lb. ground beef
2 t. Worcestershire sauce

Cover beans with water and soak overnight; drain and rinse. Return beans to pan; cover with fresh water. Bring to a boil over medium heat; reduce heat and simmer until beans are tender, 4 to 5 hours. Add tomatoes, tomato sauce and seasonings. In a skillet over medium heat, sauté onion and garlic in oil. Add ground beef and Worcestershire sauce; cook until browned and drain. Add beef mixture to beans. Simmer, uncovered, for 1-1/2 to 3 hours. Makes one gallon.

Save lots of scrubbing as soon as all the chili bowls are empty, put them to soak in a sink filled with hot, soapy water.

Our Family's Corn Muffins

Rosemary Trezza
Tarpon Springs, FL

This recipe was tested and perfected by my dad. He would make these muffins often for us. In fact, he was so proud of them he carried the recipe in his wallet. He continued to make them up until one year before he passed away at the age of 96. We continue to share Dad's recipe and enjoy these muffins continuing his family tradition.

1-3/4 c. yellow cornmeal
2-1/4 c. all-purpose flour
1 c. sugar
8 t. baking powder

1-1/4 t. salt
2 eggs, beaten
2 c. milk
3/4 c. oil

In a large bowl, combine ingredients in order listed; beat until well blended. Fill greased muffin cups 2/3 full. Bake at 425 degrees for 15 minutes, or until a toothpick tests done. Makes 1-1/2 dozen.

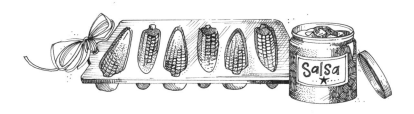

Just for fun, bake your next batch of cornbread in an
old-fashioned cornbread pan...the kind that makes
cornbread sticks shaped like ears of corn.
Kids will love 'em!

Cheddar Cheese Soup

Shannon Kreider
Elizabethtown, PA

I think this soup is ideal for serving to family & friends when you're looking for a meatless recipe everyone will love.

2 to 3 T. butter
1 c. carrot, peeled and finely chopped
1 c. onion, finely chopped
1 c. celery, finely chopped
1-1/2 t. paprika
3 c. chicken broth
8-oz. pkg. Cheddar cheese, cubed

8-oz. container refrigerated pasteurized sharp cheese spread
1/2 c. light cream
1/3 c. all-purpose flour
1 c. milk
1/2 t. Worcestershire sauce
1/8 t. pepper

Melt butter in a large saucepan over medium heat. Add vegetables; cook until onion is translucent. Stir in paprika and chicken broth; bring to a boil. Reduce heat; simmer, covered, for 10 minutes. Stir in cheeses until melted; add cream. In a small bowl, whisk together flour and milk until smooth; add to saucepan. Cook and stir until thickened. Stir in Worcestershire sauce and pepper. Heat over low heat until well blended. Serves 6.

Make your favorite soup recipe extra creamy…simply substitute an equal amount of evaporated milk for regular milk.

Family Favorite Clam Chowder

Angie Whitmore
Farmington, UT

A chowder that's so good for chasing away those winter chills.

3 to 4 c. potatoes, peeled
   and cubed
1 c. onion, diced
1 c. celery, diced
6-1/2 oz. can minced clams,
   drained and juice reserved
8-oz. bottle clam juice

3/4 c. butter
3/4 c. all-purpose flour
1 qt. half-and-half
1/2 t. sugar
1-1/2 t. salt
1/8 t. pepper

Place vegetables in a large saucepan; add reserved clam juice and bottled clam juice. Add just enough water to cover vegetables; bring to a boil over medium heat. Reduce heat; simmer, covered, until vegetables are tender, about 10 to 15 minutes. In a separate saucepan over medium heat, melt butter; whisk in flour and cook for one minute. Add half-and-half, sugar, salt and pepper, whisking until smooth. Cook on low for 3 to 4 minutes; stir into vegetable mixture. Stir in clams. Heat through, 5 to 10 minutes. Serves 8.

On warm fall days, set up harvest tables and chairs outdoors for a soup supper. Decorate with plump pumpkins, bittersweet wreaths, straw bales and scarecrows. And before the sun sets, end the day with a hayride in the country.

Bacon-Cheeseburger Soup

Darcy Geiger
Columbia City, IN

My husband just loves this hearty soup!

3 T. olive oil
2 onions, chopped
3 T. garlic, minced
4-oz. can sliced mushrooms,
    drained
1-1/2 lbs. ground beef
2 T. seasoning salt
8 redskin potatoes, cubed
4-1/2 c. water

2 cubes beef bouillon
5 c. milk or half-and-half,
    divided
2 T. all-purpose flour
3 T. bacon bits
32-oz. pkg. pasteurized process
    cheese spread, cubed
Garnish: shredded Swiss cheese

Heat oil in a large skillet over medium heat. Add onions, garlic and mushrooms; cook until onions are translucent. Add ground beef; sprinkle with seasoning salt. Cook until beef is browned; drain and set aside. Combine potatoes, water and beef bouillon in a large soup pot over medium heat. Simmer, stirring occasionally, until potatoes are tender, 10 to 15 minutes. Add 4 cups milk or half-and-half; bring to a simmer over medium heat. Add beef mixture; return to a simmer. In a small bowl, mix together flour and remaining milk until smooth. Gradually add to soup. Stir in bacon bits and cheese spread, stirring until melted and smooth. Ladle into bowls; garnish with Swiss cheese. Serves 8 to 10.

Top off a vintage tool caddy or wooden crate with
a fresh coat of paint, and it's made for holding
condiments or salt & pepper shakers.

Food for a Crowd

Company Meatloaf

1 lb. ground pork
  sausage
3 lbs. ground beef
  sirloin
1 T. dried sage
8-oz. can tomato sauce
2 c. quick-cooking
  oats, uncooked

1.35-oz. pkg. onion
  soup mix
4 eggs, beaten
2 c. evaporated milk
salt & pepper to taste

Combine all ingredients in a large bowl; mix
well. Shape into 2 loaves and place on ungreased baking sheets. Bake at 400 degrees for
30 minutes. Reduce heat to 350 degrees; bake
for an additional one hour, or until browned.

Church Bazaar Chicken à la King

Wendy Jacobs
Idaho Falls, ID

Not only is this absolutely delicious, it's oh-so perfect when you're looking for a recipe that's just right for a large get-together!

3 c. butter.
3-1/2 c. all-purpose flour
salt to taste
9 c. milk, warmed
6 lbs. cooked chicken, diced

2 4-oz. jars diced pimentos, drained
2 8-oz. pkgs. mushrooms, chopped
cooked rice or noodles

Melt butter in a large saucepan over medium heat; remove from heat. Stir in flour, a little at a time, whisking until smooth. Sprinkle with salt; gradually add warmed milk, whisking constantly. Bring to a boil, stirring until smooth and thick, about 15 to 20 minutes. Stir in chicken, pimentos and mushrooms; simmer until heated through. Serve with rice or noodles. Serves 50.

When you're planning dinner for a large group, here are some basic quantities to keep in mind each will roughly feed about 12 people:

One gallon of soup
4 pounds of boneless chicken
7-1/2 pounds of bone-in roast
2 pounds of vegetables

Cherry-Glazed Baked Ham

Jennifer Oglesby
Brownsville, IN

This recipe is for a great baked ham that I love to take to church socials. It's so good, I never come home with leftovers!

12 to 15-lb. fully-cooked bone-in ham 1 t. allspice	2-ltr. bottle cola 3/4 c. cherry jelly 1/4 c. orange juice

Place ham fat-side up in a shallow roasting pan. With a knife, score a diamond pattern into top of ham. Sprinkle with allspice; rub into ham. Pour cola into pan. Bake at 325 degrees for one hour and 15 minutes, basting with pan juices every 15 minutes. Combine jelly and orange juice in a saucepan over medium heat, stirring until melted. Brush ham with jelly glaze. Bake for an additional 15 to 30 minutes, basting with pan juices every 15 minutes, until a thermometer inserted into the thickest part of ham registers 140 degrees. Remove ham from oven; let stand 30 minutes before carving. Serves 15 to 20.

If you have a favorite recipe you want to share, but it has a small serving size, don't worry. Most recipes can successfully be tripled or even made up to four times the serving amount of the original recipe.

Lisa's Best-Ever Lasagna

Lisa Hill
Salinas, CA

If you can start this the day before, it's even better.

2 24-oz. jars spaghetti sauce
16-oz. can tomato purée
15-oz. can diced tomatoes,
    drained
1/4 c. sugar
1 onion, diced
1 red pepper, chopped
1 yellow pepper, chopped
2 8-oz. cans whole black
    olives, drained
1 clove garlic, minced

1 t. dried oregano
2 12-oz. pkgs. shredded
    mozzarella cheese
8-oz. pkg. shredded provolone
    cheese
2 16-oz. pkgs. lasagna
    noodles, cooked
1 c. grated Parmesan cheese
12-oz. pkg. shredded Monterey
    Jack cheese

Combine first 10 ingredients in a large stockpot over medium heat.
Simmer for one hour. Mix together cheeses; set aside. Spray two,
14"x11" baking pans with non-stick vegetable spray. Spread a thin
layer of sauce in pans. Layer lasagna noodles, sauce and cheese,
ending with cheese. Repeat layers for a total of 3 layers. Bake at
350 degrees for 30 to 40 minutes, until golden and bubbly. Serves
25 to 30.

If you do decide to double or
triple a recipe, keep this in mind...
never double or triple the amount
of salt. When increasing the
recipe servings, add only
1-1/2 times the amount of
salt originally called for
and then taste.

Mama Ricciuti's Spaghetti Gravy
Victoria McElroy
Northbrook, IL

My grandfathers and father were born in Italy, and this recipe has been passed down from them.

2 T. olive oil
2-lb. pork shoulder roast
2 lbs. hot Italian ground pork
  sausage
8 cloves garlic, coarsely chopped
1/2 c. red wine or beef broth
4 28-oz. cans tomato sauce

18-oz. can tomato paste
4 plum tomatoes, chopped
salt and pepper to taste
2 16-oz. pkgs. spaghetti,
  cooked
Garnish: grated Parmesan
  cheese

Heat oil in a large saucepan over medium heat. Add pork roast, sausage and garlic. Cook until roast and sausage are browned; drain. Add wine or broth; cook for one minute and set aside. Combine tomato sauce and paste in a Dutch oven; stir in tomatoes. Add meat mixture, remaining wine or broth, salt and pepper. Simmer over medium heat for 2 to 2-1/2 hours. Spoon over hot pasta; garnish with Parmesan cheese. Serves 10 to 15.

When you need to chill lots of juice boxes, bottled water, cartons of milk or cans of soda, you'll find they chill more quickly on ice than in the refrigerator. Just add beverages to an ice-filled cooler or galvanized tub...you'll save valuable refrigerator space too!

Easy French Dip Sandwiches

Kathleen White
Cato, NY

My husband is the pastor of our church and we regularly host meals with our family of 10 and the congregation. This recipe is one of our newest favorites and feeds a crowd!

4 lbs. stew beef, cubed
2 onions
4 cloves garlic
2 10-1/2 oz. cans beef broth

4 c. water
4 t. beef bouillon granules
18 to 20 sandwich buns, split

Combine all ingredients except buns in a slow cooker. Cover and cook on low setting for 8 to 10 hours. Discard onions and garlic. Shred beef and spoon onto buns. Serve with beef juices from slow cooker for dipping. Serves 18 to 20.

On days when warmth is the most important need of the human heart, the kitchen is the place you can find it.
–E.B. White

Shredded Pork Sandwiches

Roberta Goll
Chesterfield, MI

*Pass the coleslaw...perfect with these tender,
shredded sandwiches!*

8-lb. pork shoulder roast
1.35-oz. pkg. onion soup mix
1 c. barbecue sauce

12-oz. can beer or
  1-1/2 c. beef broth
40 sandwich buns, split

Combine all ingredients except buns in a slow cooker. Cover and cook on low setting for 8 hours. Remove roast from cooking liquid and refrigerate liquid. Using 2 forks, shred roast. Skim fat from surface of cooled liquid. Stir in cooking liquid to taste over shredded meat; mix well. Spoon onto buns; serve remaining sauce on the side. Serves 40.

Church socials are a great time to have mini classes, only 15 minutes each, on a variety of topics. Once your class is complete, rotate to another one. Interesting class topics might be the basics of first aid, tracing your family history, simple scrapbooking and food storage.

Church Supper Tuna Bake

Stephanie Mayer
Portsmouth, VA

An old-fashioned favorite that everyone loves.

1/4 c. butter
3/4 c. green pepper, diced
3 c. celery, sliced
2 onions, chopped
3 10-3/4 oz. cans cream of
   mushroom soup
2 c. milk
12-oz. pkg. American cheese,
   cubed

24-oz. pkg. medium egg
   noodles, cooked
1-1/2 c. mayonnaise
4-oz. can chopped pimentos,
   drained
3 9-1/2 oz. cans tuna, drained
1 c. slivered almonds, toasted

Melt butter in a skillet over medium heat. Add pepper, celery and onions; sauté for 10 minutes, or until tender. Combine soup and milk in a large stockpot; add vegetable mixture and heat through. Stir in cheese until melted. Mix together cooked noodles and 2 cups soup mixture; toss to coat. Spread in 2 lightly greased 13"x9" baking pans. Combine remaining soup mixture with mayonnaise, pimentos and tuna. Pour over noodles and mix gently; sprinkle with almonds. Bake, uncovered, at 375 degrees for 35 to 40 minutes. Serves 25.

Save time by cooking a casserole ahead, it's easy! Line the casserole dish with aluminum foil, leaving a 2-inch overhang around edges. Add casserole ingredients, bake as directed, cool and freeze, uncovered. When completely frozen, lift the casserole out using the aluminum foil overhang. Cover and freeze. To thaw, simply place in the casserole dish it was originally baked in.

Old-Fashioned Ham Loaf

Kate Scott
Mulberry, IN

My mother-in-law, Wilma Scott, is co-chairperson for her church's annual dinner held in April each year. All of the food they serve is homemade and feeds a crowd of 300!

2-1/2 lbs. ground ham
2-1/2 lbs. ground pork
2 c. milk
4 eggs, beaten
2 c. bread crumbs

2 c. brown sugar, packed
1 c. vinegar
1 c. water
2 t. mustard

Combine ham and pork; blend well. Add milk, eggs and bread crumbs; mix well. Shape into 20 individual loaves and arrange on lightly greased baking sheets; set aside. Mix together brown sugar, vinegar, water and mustard in a saucepan over medium heat. Heat through and spoon over loaves. Bake at 350 degrees for 1-1/2 to 2 hours. Makes 20 servings.

Why not call an activities committee to help plan church get-togethers? They can organize all the to-do's... creating flyers or sending invitations, finding friends to lend a hand cooking or serving, helping with table & chair set-up and take-down, even decorating.

Slow-Cooker Roast for Tacos

Dana Thompson
Delaware, OH

Don't forget to offer all the tasty taco toppers...shredded cheese,
sour cream, lettuce, tomatoes, onions and salsa. Olé!

4 to 5-lb. beef chuck roast
1 T. chili powder
1 t. ground cumin
1 t. onion powder

1 t. garlic powder
2 14-1/2 oz. cans Mexican-
    style stewed tomatoes
taco shells

Place roast in a large slow cooker; sprinkle with spices. Add tomatoes
with juice around the roast. Cover and cook on low setting for 8 to
10 hours. Using 2 forks, shred roast and return to slow cooker. Spoon
into taco shells. Makes 10 cups.

Easy, breezy decorating ideas for a summertime church social.
Fill kids' brightly colored sand pails with flowers and a sprinkle
of sand...centerpieces in a snap. Add a mix & match of sunny
colored plastic plates and cups and you're all set!

Food for a Crowd

Company Meatloaf

Phyllis Peters
Three Rivers, MI

A tried & true recipe sure to please.

1 lb. ground pork sausage
3 lbs. ground beef sirloin
1 T. dried sage
2 c. quick-cooking oats,
    uncooked

8-oz. can tomato sauce
1.35-oz. pkg. onion soup mix
4 eggs, beaten
2 c. evaporated milk
salt and pepper to taste

Combine all ingredients in a large bowl; mix well. Shape into
2 loaves and place on ungreased baking sheets. Bake at 400 degrees
for 30 minutes. Reduce heat to 350 degrees; bake for an additional
one hour, or until browned. Makes 15 servings.

Crowd-Pleasing Chili

Lane McLeod
Siloam Springs, AR

This recipe is used for our Christmas parade
and town lighting ceremony.

5 lbs. ground beef
5 10-3/4 oz. cans tomato soup
Optional: 5 15-1/2 oz. cans
    chili beans
2 1.35-oz. pkgs. onion
    soup mix

5 t. garlic, minced
3 T. chili powder
2-1/2 c. water
Garnish: shredded Cheddar
    cheese
saltine crackers or corn chips

Brown ground beef in a Dutch oven over medium heat; drain. Add
remaining ingredients except cheese and crackers or corn chips;
simmer for 1-1/2 hours. Sprinkle with cheese; serve with crackers
or corn chips. Serves 20 to 25.

Super Cornbread Salad

Shannon Wells
Harrison, AR

This salad is always a hit at church potlucks and school luncheons. People usually don't know what it is and after they try it, they love it and ask for the recipe!

2 8-1/2 oz. pkgs. cornbread
   mix, prepared
1-1/2 c. mayonnaise-type
   salad dressing
1/2 c. sweet pickle juice
4 tomatoes, chopped

1 green pepper, chopped
1 red onion, chopped
3 stalks celery, chopped
3 whole sweet pickles, finely
   chopped
3-oz. pkg. bacon bits

Combine cornbread mixes and prepare according to package directions; cool and set aside. Mix together salad dressing and pickle juice; set aside. Crumble 1/3 of cornbread into a large bowl. Layer half of tomatoes, pepper, onion, celery and pickles on top in that order. Top with half of bacon bits; spread with half of salad dressing mixture. Repeat layers, ending with cornbread and then bacon on top. Chill in refrigerator until ready to serve. Serves 20 to 25.

Following dinner, settle in to enjoy a talent show or movie night. Invite everyone to bring beanbag chairs, blankets or quilts and keep the menu simple...hot dogs, potato chips, popcorn and sodas.

Herbed New Potato Salad

Jo Ann
Gooseberry Patch

*The combination of sage, shallots and thyme
really dresses up a crowd favorite.*

5 lbs. new potatoes
1 bunch fresh sage
1/2 c. olive oil, divided
salt and pepper to taste
1/4 c. red wine vinegar

3 T. shallots, finely chopped
1 t. fresh thyme, minced
Garnish: fresh sage leaves,
  sprigs fresh thyme

Place potatoes and sage on a 15"x10" jelly-roll pan; drizzle with
1/4 cup oil and toss gently. Bake at 450 degrees for 35 to 40 minutes,
until golden and tender; cool. Halve potatoes and place in a serving
bowl; sprinkle with salt and pepper. Crumble roasted sage leaves over
potatoes. Whisk together remaining oil, vinegar, shallots and thyme;
drizzle over potatoes. Toss to coat. Garnish with fresh sage and thyme
sprigs. Chill. Serves 15.

Celebrate Friendship Day, the first Sunday in August,
by inviting friends over for dinner!

Grandma's Baked Mac & Cheese

Rebecca LaMere
Yulee, FL

*My grandma is famous at her church for this recipe and is
always asked to bring it for church suppers or luncheons.*

3 12-oz. pkgs. jumbo elbow
  macaroni, uncooked
1-1/2 c. butter, divided
1 to 1-1/2 c. all-purpose flour
4 to 6 c. milk

1-1/2 lbs. pasteurized process
  cheese spread, cubed
16-oz. pkg. shredded sharp
  Cheddar cheese
1-1/2 c. soft bread crumbs

Measure 10 cups macaroni; prepare according to package directions.
Reserve remaining uncooked macaroni for use in another recipe. Pour
macaroni into a very large bowl; set aside. Melt 3/4 cup butter in a
saucepan over medium heat; whisk in one cup flour. If sauce is thin,
add more flour. Add 4 cups milk; whisk to blend well. If needed, add
more milk. Stir in cheese spread until melted. Add shredded cheese;
mix until melted. Pour sauce over macaroni; mix well. Spread mixture
in a lightly greased 15"x12" baking pan. Melt remaining butter in a
saucepan. Stir in bread crumbs; mix until butter is absorbed. Sprinkle
over macaroni. Bake at 350 degrees for about 30 minutes, until
golden and bubbly. Serves 25 to 30.

This year, host a Trunk or Treat in your church parking lot
for little ones. Cars pull into parking spots, then pop their
decorated trunks open as little clowns and cowboys, pirates
and princesses go from car-to-car trick-or-treating. Afterward,
bring everyone inside for a warming supper served family style.

Food for a Crowd

Loaded Mashed Potato Casserole
Nancy Girard
Chesapeake, VA

Filled with so many good things!

5-1/2 c. mashed potatoes
1/2 c. milk
8-oz. pkg. cream cheese,
  softened
8-oz. container sour cream
2 t. dried parsley

1 t. garlic salt
1/4 t. nutmeg
3/4 c. shredded Cheddar cheese
12 slices bacon, crisply cooked
  and crumbled

Beat together all ingredients except cheese and bacon until smooth and creamy. Spoon into a lightly greased 13"x9" baking pan; sprinkle with cheese and bacon. Cover and bake at 350 degrees for 30 minutes, or until heated through. Serves 12.

Paula's Corn Casserole
Paula Marchesi
Lenhartsville, PA

A must-have for any get-together.

2 sweet onions, thinly sliced
1/2 c. butter
8-oz. container sour cream
1/2 c. milk
1/2 t. dill weed
1/4 t. salt

8-oz. pkg. shredded Cheddar
  cheese, divided
1 egg, beaten
14-3/4 oz. can creamed corn
8-1/2 oz. pkg. cornbread mix
4 drops hot pepper sauce

In a large skillet over medium heat, sauté onions in butter until tender. Combine sour cream, milk, dill weed and salt in a small bowl; stir in one cup cheese. Stir into onion mixture. Remove from heat; set aside. Combine egg, corn, cornbread mix and pepper sauce in a large bowl. Spread in a greased 13"x9" baking pan; spoon onion mixture over top. Sprinkle with remaining cheese. Bake, uncovered, at 350 degrees for 40 to 45 minutes, until lightly golden. Let stand 10 minutes before serving. Serves 12 to 15.

Broccoli-Bacon Raisin Salad

Kathleen White
Cato, NY

*You just can't miss with this salad, everyone really loves it.
You can easily substitute sweetened dried cranberries for
the raisins and add chopped cauliflower too...delicious!*

4 bunches broccoli, chopped
2 c. bacon bits
3 c. raisins
1/2 c. onion, chopped
Optional: shredded Cheddar
   cheese to taste

Optional: sunflower kernels
   to taste
1/2 c. sugar
1/4 c. vinegar
1-1/2 c. mayonnaise

Combine broccoli, bacon bits, raisins and onion in a large bowl.
Add cheese and sunflower kernels, if using. Stir together remaining
ingredients. Pour over broccoli mixture; mix well. Cover and
refrigerate until ready to serve. Serves 18 to 24.

Hand out plastic zipping bags filled with crayons,
mini coloring books and stickers to little ones...
they'll be happy creating crayon masterpieces while
waiting for dinner or an activity to begin.

Food for a Crowd

Chilled Pesto Salad

Shirl Parsons
Cape Carteret, NC

*Take this to your next church supper and
you will go home with an empty dish!*

2 16-oz. pkgs. elbow macaroni,
  uncooked
5 16-oz. pkgs. frozen Italian
  vegetables
3 c. green onion, thinly sliced
4 7-3/4 oz. cans black olives,
  drained and sliced
2 c. fresh parsley, chopped
1 c. tomato paste

1 c. dried basil
4 to 6 T. garlic, chopped
1/3 c. oil
1 c. vinegar
5-1/2 oz. container grated
  Parmesan cheese
2 qts. plain yogurt
2 lbs. tomatoes, chopped

Cook macaroni according to package directions until just tender.
Drain and transfer to a large bowl; cool. Cook vegetables until just
tender. Drain and cut into bite-size pieces, if necessary; cool. Add
vegetables, onion, olives and parsley to macaroni; mix well and
set aside. Combine tomato paste, basil, garlic to taste and oil in a
blender or food processor. Process until smooth. Add vinegar, cheese
and yogurt; blend to mix well. Pour over macaroni mixture. Stir in
tomatoes; mix well. Chill. Serves 50.

Nestle serving bowls of chilled salads in larger bowls filled with
crushed ice...sure to keep salads cool, crisp and refreshing.

Rainbow Gelatin Salad

Kendra Fletcher
Denair, CA

Our small church of 200 people has a potluck lunch every Sunday after service. The children far outnumber the adults, making for a happy, joyful lunch gathering. Children and adults alike love the creamy layers and combination of flavors in this salad.

6-oz. pkg. orange gelatin mix	6-oz. pkg. lemon gelatin mix
8 c. boiling water, divided	6-oz. pkg. lime gelatin mix
4 c. sour cream, divided	6-oz. pkg. cherry gelatin mix

Dissolve orange gelatin in 2 cups boiling water. Combine 1/2 cup prepared orange gelatin with one cup sour cream; mix well. Reserve remaining prepared orange gelatin. Pour gelatin-sour cream mixture into an ungreased 13"x9" baking pan; chill until set. Pour remaining prepared orange gelatin over top; chill until firm. Repeat all instructions with each flavor of gelatin. Chill until set. Serves 24.

Along with all the tasty food, don't forget you'll need lots of the basics, so stock up on utensils, napkins, cups, plates, tablecloths, serving utensils, baskets for rolls, bowls, butter dishes and pitchers.

Mandarin Orange Salad

Liz Plotnick-Snay
Gooseberry Patch

*Quick & easy to prepare, this salad is delicious
topped with a sweet dressing.*

4 c. green or red leaf lettuce,
   torn into bite-size pieces
2 15-oz. cans mandarin
   oranges, drained

1/2 c. walnut pieces, toasted
1/2 red onion, sliced

Combine all ingredients in a salad bowl. Just before serving, toss with desired amount of Raspberry Vinaigrette. Serves 8.

Raspberry Vinaigrette:

1/3 c. raspberry vinegar
1/3 c. seedless red raspberry
   jam
1 t. coriander or ground cumin

1/2 t. salt
1/4 t. pepper
3/4 c. olive oil

Combine all ingredients except olive oil in a blender. Process on high until blended; gradually add oil. Cover and chill.

When lots of friends get together, it can be the best time for a service activity. Why not help plant or weed a garden, gather and donate gently used clothing, tidy up the local park or stack firewood for a neighbor?

Dutch Apple Pie

Jo Ann
Gooseberry Patch

This homemade pie is a traditional favorite.

2-1/4 c. plus 1/3 c. all-purpose
   flour, divided
3/4 t. salt
2/3 c. butter-flavored shortening
8 to 10 T. cold water, divided

2/3 c. sugar
1 t. cinnamon
3-1/2 lbs. Granny Smith apples,
   peeled, cored and thinly
   sliced

Combine 2-1/4 cups flour and salt in a large bowl. Cut in shortening until mixture resembles coarse crumbs. Sprinkle one tablespoon cold water over part of flour mixture; gently toss with a fork. Push moistened dough to side of bowl. Repeat, using one tablespoon water at a time, until all flour mixture is moistened. Gently knead the dough until a ball forms. In a separate large bowl, combine remaining flour and cinnamon. Add apples, tossing to coat; set aside. On a lightly floured surface, roll out dough into a 19"x13" rectangle. Wrap around rolling pin; transfer to an aluminum foil-lined 15"x10" jelly-roll pan. Pat up sides of pan. Trim dough to 1/2 inch beyond edge of pan. Fold dough edge over; crimp as desired. Spoon apple mixture onto dough; sprinkle with crumb topping. Bake at 375 degrees for 40 to 45 minutes, until apples are tender. Cut into squares. Serves 24.

Crumb Topping:

1 c. quick-cooking oats,
   uncooked
1 c. brown sugar, packed

1/2 c. all-purpose flour
1/2 c. butter
1/2 c. chopped pecans

Stir together oats, brown sugar and flour; cut in butter until mixture resembles coarse crumbs. Stir in pecans.

Food for a Crowd

Pioneer Blueberry Buckle

Michelle Fareri
Haddon Heights, NJ

Simple to make, feeds a crowd and tastes so good!
I use fresh blueberries for this dessert.

5 c. all-purpose flour, divided
1-1/2 c. sugar
1/2 c. butter, softened
2 eggs

1 c. milk
4 t. baking powder
1 t. salt
4 c. blueberries

Combine 4 cups flour and remaining ingredients except blueberries; mix well and set aside. Gently toss blueberries with one cup flour; discard any remaining flour. Add blueberry mixture to flour mixture. Spread into a greased and floured 13"x9" baking pan. Sprinkle with topping. Bake at 375 degrees for about one hour, until golden and toothpick tests clean. Serves 20.

Topping:

1 c. sugar
1 c. brown sugar, packed
1-1/3 c. all-purpose flour

2 t. cinnamon
1 c. butter, softened
Optional: 1 c. chopped nuts

Mix together sugars, flour and cinnamon; cut in butter to resemble coarse crumbs. Stir in nuts, if using.

Lots of communities celebrate Pioneer Day on July 24...
a fun-filled family event! Dressing up pioneer-style is optional,
but be sure to bring out lots of old-fashioned games like push
the potato, egg-in-the-spoon and 3-legged races. After dinner,
settle in for some story-telling and fiddle playing.

185

Peanut Butter Texas Sheet Cake

Kathi Rostash
Nevada, OH

*I made this for a church get-together and had
many requests for the recipe...so will you!*

2 c. all-purpose flour
2 c. sugar
1/2 t. salt
1 t. baking soda
1 c. butter

1 c. water
1/4 c. creamy peanut butter
2 eggs, beaten
1 t. vanilla extract
1/2 c. buttermilk

Sift together flour, sugar, salt and baking soda in a large bowl; set aside. Combine butter, water and peanut butter in a saucepan over medium heat; bring to a boil. Add to flour mixture and mix well; set aside. Combine eggs, vanilla and buttermilk; add to peanut butter mixture. Spread into a greased 15"x10" jelly-roll pan. Bake at 350 degrees for 15 to 20 minutes, until it springs back when gently touched. Spread Peanut Butter Icing over warm cake. Makes 15 to 20 servings.

Peanut Butter Icing:

1/2 c. butter
1/4 c. creamy peanut butter
1/3 c. plus 1 T. milk

16-oz. pkg. powdered sugar
1 t. vanilla extract

Combine butter, peanut butter and milk in a saucepan over medium heat; bring to a boil. Remove from heat; stir in powdered sugar and vanilla to a spreading consistency.

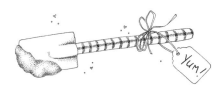

Jot down a date and enjoy a cake walk...as much fun now
as they were in Grandma's day!

Farmgirl Chocolate Chippers

Mary Murray
Mt. Vernon, OH

Whether you're looking for a treat to tote to girls' camp,
or to share with the little ones in the church nursery,
this recipe makes a bunch!

2 c. butter, softened
2 c. sugar
2 c. brown sugar, packed
4 eggs, beaten
2 t. vanilla extract
5 c. long-cooking oats,
   uncooked
4 c. all-purpose flour

1 t. salt
2 t. baking powder
2 t. baking soda
2 12-oz. pkgs. semi-sweet
   chocolate chips
7-oz. pkg. chocolate candy
   bar, grated
3 c. chopped nuts

Blend together butter, sugar and brown sugar in a large bowl; mix well. Add eggs and vanilla; set aside. Working in batches, process oats in a blender or food processor until powdery. Combine oats, flour, salt, baking powder and baking soda in a large bowl; mix into butter mixture. Stir in chocolate chips, grated chocolate and nuts. Form into golf ball-size balls; arrange on ungreased baking sheets 2 inches apart. Bake at 375 degrees for 6 minutes. Makes 10 dozen.

It is almost impossible to double or triple recipe ingredients for cakes, cookies or pie dough. It's best to rely on a recipe that feeds a bunch, or prepare several batches of a single recipe until you have the quantity you need.

Pink Cranberry Freeze

Molly Wilson
Box Elder, SD

I grew up in Texas where summers are quite hot and whenever we were going to a church social, my mom was always asked to make this frozen treat.

1-1/2 c. cream cheese, softened
1/4 c. mayonnaise
1/4 c. sugar
2 16-oz. cans whole-berry
   cranberry sauce

2 8-oz. cans crushed pineapple
1 c. chopped pecans or walnuts
2 c. whipping cream
1 c. powdered sugar
2 t. vanilla extract

Mix together cream cheese, mayonnaise and sugar. Stir in fruit and nuts; set aside. Beat together whipping cream, powdered sugar and vanilla. Fold into cream cheese mixture. Pour into 2 ungreased 9"x5" loaf pans. Freeze for at least 6 hours. Slice to serve. Serves 25.

Serving frosty lemonade or fruity punch?
Plan on 6 to 8 gallons to quench 100 thirsty friends!

Ice Cream Socials & Bake Sales

Caramel Sauce

1 c. brown sugar,
packed

1/4 c. butter
1/4 c. whipping cream

Combine all ingredients in a small saucepan over medium heat. Bring to a boil, stirring constantly. Boil for one minute. Remove from heat; cool. Chill for one hour. Makes about one cup.

Yellow Cake $7.00

Berry Pie $5.00

Cream Cake $8.00

The Easiest Brownies Ever

Tammy Rowe
Bellevue, OH

No bake sale is complete without brownies!

2 c. milk
3.9-oz. pkg. instant chocolate
    pudding mix
18-1/4 oz. pkg. chocolate
    cake mix

12-oz. pkg. semi-sweet
    chocolate chips
Garnish: powdered sugar

Combine milk and pudding mix in a large bowl; add cake mix and stir until well blended. Stir in chocolate chips; spread in a greased 15"x10" jelly-roll pan. Bake at 350 degrees for 30 minutes, or until set in the middle. Cool; cut into bars and sprinkle with powdered sugar. Makes 12 to 15.

Before adding the brownie batter, line your baking dish with aluminum foil, then grease the foil. Once the brownies have baked and cooled, they'll lift right out of the pan.

Granny's Chocolate Fudge Cookies

Karen Adams
Cincinnati, OH

My grandmother used to make these for church dinners.
The food was awesome, especially these cookies!

2 6-oz. pkgs. semi-sweet
    chocolate chips
1/4 c. butter
14-oz. can sweetened
    condensed milk

1 t. vanilla extract
1 c. all-purpose flour
1 c. chopped nuts

Heat chocolate chips, butter and condensed milk in a microwave-safe bowl on high setting until melted, stirring every 30 seconds. Add vanilla, flour and nuts. Drop by teaspoonfuls onto greased baking sheets. Bake at 350 degrees for 7 minutes. Cool on wire racks. Makes 5 to 6 dozen.

When you're packaging cookies for a bake sale, be creative! Stack Granny's Chocolate Fudge Cookies in tall glasses and add a whimsical tag that reads, "Just add milk!"

Razz-Ma-Tazz Bars

Kimberly Hancock
Murrieta, CA

A sure-fire bake sale winner...you can
substitute any kind of jam you like.

1/2 c. butter
2 c. white chocolate chips,
   divided
2 eggs
1/2 c. sugar

1 c. all-purpose flour
1/2 t. salt
1/2 t. almond extract
1/2 c. seedless raspberry jam
1/4 c. sliced almonds, toasted

Melt butter in a large microwave-safe bowl on high setting for one minute; stir. Add one cup chocolate chips; let stand without stirring. In a large mixing bowl, beat eggs until foamy. Add sugar; using an electric mixer on high speed, beat for 5 minutes. Stir in butter mixture. Add flour, salt and extract; mix at low speed until combined. Spread 2/3 of batter in a greased and sugared 9"x9" baking pan. Bake at 325 degrees for 15 to 17 minutes, until golden around edges; remove to a wire rack. Heat jam in a small microwave-safe bowl on high for 30 seconds; stir. Spread jam over warm crust. Stir remaining chocolate chips into remaining batter. Dollop batter by tablespoonfuls over jam; sprinkle with almonds. Bake for an additional 25 to 30 minutes, until edges are golden. Cool completely in pan on wire rack. Slice into bars. Makes 16.

A balanced diet is a cookie in each hand!

–Unknown

Black Forest Cherry Bars

Judy Voster
Neenah, WI

These rich bars are a hit at our potluck dinners at church.

3 21-oz. cans cherry pie filling, divided
18-1/2 oz. pkg. chocolate cake mix
1/4 c. oil
3 eggs

1/4 c. cherry-flavored brandy or cherry juice
6-oz. pkg. semi-sweet chocolate chips
Optional: whipped topping

Refrigerate 2 cans of pie filling until chilled. Using an electric mixer, beat together remaining can of pie filling, cake mix, oil, eggs and brandy or cherry juice until well mixed. Stir in chocolate chips. Pour into a lightly greased 13"x9" baking pan. Bake at 350 degrees for 25 to 30 minutes, until toothpick tests clean; chill. Spread chilled pie filling evenly over cake. Serve with whipped topping, if desired. Serves 10 to 12.

Use Grandma's secret for keeping cookies moist...
slip a slice of bread into the cookie jar!

Divine Lemon Cupcakes

Jackie Smulski
Lyons, IL

Tangy and slightly sweet...yummy!

2/3 c. shortening
1 c. sugar
3 eggs
1-2/3 c. all-purpose flour

2-1/2 t. baking powder
1/2 t. salt
2/3 c. milk
1 T. lemon zest

In a large bowl, blend shortening and sugar. Add eggs, one at a time, beating well after each addition. Set aside. Combine flour, baking powder and salt in a separate bowl; add to shortening mixture alternately with milk. Mix well; stir in lemon zest. Fill paper-lined muffin cups 2/3 full. Sprinkle topping by rounded 1/2 teaspoonfuls over each cupcake. Bake at 350 degrees for 20 to 24 minutes, or until a toothpick comes out clean. Cool for 10 minutes before removing from tins to wire racks. Makes about 1-1/4 dozen.

Topping:

1/4 c. sugar
1 T. lemon zest

1/8 t. nutmeg

Stir together ingredients in a small bowl.

While you're at a tag sale or flea market, keep an eye out for vintage cookie cutters. With their one-of-a-kind shapes, they're sure to add lots of whimsy to cut-out cookies.

Orange Puff Cupcakes

Heather Roberts
Quebec, Canada

This is an old-fashioned recipe handed down from my grandmother. The ladies at our annual church social recommend this recipe for our bake sale and tea table.

1/3 c. margarine
1 c. sugar
2 eggs, beaten
1-3/4 c. all-purpose flour
1 T. baking powder

1/2 c. frozen orange juice
   concentrate, thawed
Optional: zest of 1 orange,
   frosting

Beat together margarine and sugar in a mixing bowl; add eggs. Combine flour and baking powder; add alternately with orange juice to sugar mixture. Stir in zest, if using. Fill paper-lined muffin cups 2/3 full. Bake at 375 degrees for 15 minutes. Cool and spread with frosting, if desired. Makes one dozen.

A large blackboard makes a great bake sale sign. Pull out lots of colorful chalk to jot down the hours you'll be set up, goodie prices and what your fundraiser is for.

Homemade Ice Cream

Jill Valentine
Jackson, TN

Nothing, simply nothing, is as good as homemade ice cream.

2 eggs, beaten
1 c. sugar
1/4 t. salt

2-1/2 c. whipping cream
2 c. half-and-half
2-1/4 t. vanilla extract

Combine first 5 ingredients in a heavy saucepan over medium-low heat, stirring constantly, until mixture is thick enough to coat the back of a spoon and reaches at least 160 degrees. Remove from heat. Set pan in an ice-filled bowl; stir. Cover and refrigerate overnight or add vanilla, pour into ice cream maker and freeze according to manufacturer's directions. Serves 12.

Quick & Easy Hot Fudge Sauce

Linda Reynolds
Cut Bank, MT

Tried & true, this delicious recipe was passed down from my grandmother and mom. It's been a favorite for decades and I've been known to multiply it 12 times to make banana splits for the cross country team my husband coaches.

1/3 c. milk
1/3 c. baking cocoa

1/3 c. shortening
1 c. sugar

Mix together all ingredients in a heavy saucepan over medium heat. Bring to a boil, stirring with a wooden spoon. Boil for 30 seconds; remove from heat and serve. May be refrigerated and used later. Makes 1-1/2 to 2 cups.

A sweet shake for one! Crunch up your favorite candy bar and freeze for 10 minutes. Add to a blender along with 2-1/2 cups vanilla ice cream and 1/4 cup milk. Blend on medium speed for 30 seconds, stir, blend 30 seconds longer...enjoy!

Rocky Road Pops

Pat Habiger
Spearville, KS

An all-time favorite flavor in a popsicle!

3.4-oz. pkg. cook & serve
   chocolate pudding mix
2-1/2 c. chocolate milk
1/2 c. mini semi-sweet
   chocolate chips

3/4 c. mini marshmallows
Optional: 1/2 c. chopped
   walnuts
9 3-oz. paper cups
9 wooden treat sticks

Combine pudding mix and milk in a medium saucepan; cook and stir over medium heat until bubbly. Pour into a large bowl; let cool slightly. Cover surface with plastic wrap and refrigerate for one hour. Stir in chocolate chips, marshmallows and nuts, if using. Spoon about 1/3 cup of mixture into each paper cup; cover each cup with a piece of aluminum foil. Make a small slit in center of foil with a knife tip; insert a wooden stick. Freeze for 4 hours, or until firm. To serve, let pops stand at room temperature for 10 minutes; remove foil and tear the paper cup from each pop. Makes 9 pops.

Offer a sampler plate at your bake sale...just right for those who want a taste of everything. Fill the plate with a variety of cookies, brownies, fudge and even a cupcake.

Strawberry Cream Cheese Pie

Rhonda Phillips
Sand Springs, OK

My grandmother was a very talented lady who really knew about baking. This was such a favorite at church bake sales that everyone would always ask how many pies she would be bringing!

3-oz. pkg. cream cheese,
   softened
1/2 c. powdered sugar
1/2 t. vanilla extract
1/4 t. almond extract
1/2 c. whipping cream, whipped
9-inch pie crust

1/3 c. sugar
2 T. cornstarch
1/3 c. water
1/3 c. grenadine syrup
1 T. lemon juice
2 c. strawberries, hulled

Combine cream cheese, powdered sugar and extracts in a large bowl; beat until smooth and creamy. Fold in whipped cream; spread evenly over pie crust. Chill for several hours. Combine sugar and cornstarch in a small saucepan; add water slowly, stirring until smooth. Add grenadine and lemon juice. Cook over medium heat. stirring constantly, until thick and clear; cool and add strawberries, mixing gently. Spread berries over chilled mixture. Chill before serving. Serves 8.

Offer whole pies as well as slices at your church bake sale. Served up with a fork, slices are ideal to enjoy right now, while a whole pie will be perfect for dessert tonight.

Tennessee Fudge Pie

Dusty Jones
Paxton, IL

*My mama has always made this pie for Thanksgiving and
people request it for church socials, parties and
family suppers. It's a chocolate lover's dream!*

2 eggs, beaten
1/2 c. butter, melted and cooled
1/4 c. baking cocoa
1/4 c. all-purpose flour
1 c. sugar
2 t. vanilla extract

1/3 c. semi-sweet chocolate
    chips
1/3 c. chopped pecans
9-inch pie crust
Optional: whipped cream,
    chocolate curls

Beat together eggs and butter in a large bowl. Add remaining
ingredients except pie crust; mix well. Pour into pie crust. Bake at
350 degrees for 25 minutes, or until firm. Garnish, if desired. Serves 8.

Add a dollop of homemade whipped cream to pie and
cake slices...it's a snap to make and tastes so much better
than store-bought. In a chilled bowl, combine one cup heavy
cream with 1/4 cup powdered sugar and one teaspoon
vanilla extract; beat until stiff peaks form.

Banana Bread Muffins

Bonnie Fuller
Lead, SD

This recipe brings back many hectic 4-H
pre-achievement day baking binges!

1 c. oil	1/2 c. whole-wheat flour
1 c. sugar	1/2 t. salt
2 eggs, beaten	2 to 3 T. lemon juice
3 bananas, mashed	2 t. baking soda
1-1/2 c. all-purpose flour	1 c. semi-sweet chocolate chips

Blend together oil and sugar in a large bowl; add eggs and bananas
and set aside. Mix together flours and salt; stir into oil mixture. Add
lemon juice and baking soda; fold in chocolate chips. Spoon
into greased muffin cups filling 2/3 full. Bake at 350 degrees for
25 minutes. Makes about 2 dozen.

Poppy Seed Mini Muffins

Donna Rasheed
Greer, SC

Split and top with a tiny scoop of ice cream for little ones.

2 c. all-purpose flour	8-oz. pkg. shredded Cheddar
1 T. brown sugar, packed	cheese
1-1/2 t. baking powder	1 c. buttermilk
1/8 t. salt	1 egg, beaten
1/4 c. butter, softened	2 to 3 T. poppy seed

Sift together first 4 ingredients. Mix in butter; stir in cheese. Add
buttermilk and egg; mix just until moistened. Spoon into greased
mini muffin cups to fill 1/2 full; sprinkle to taste with poppy seed.
Bake at 400 degrees for 10 to 12 minutes, or until tops are golden.
Makes 3 dozen.

Bishop's Bread

Nola Coons
Gooseberry Patch

This sweet bread filled with cherries, chocolate and nuts, is said to have been served to traveling clergy in the 19th century.

1 egg
1/2 c. sugar
1/4 c. oil
1 t. vanilla extract
1 c. buttermilk
2 c. all-purpose flour
1/2 t. baking soda

1/2 t. salt
1/2 c. chopped pecans
1/2 c. maraschino cherries,
  chopped
1/2 c. raisins
1/2 c. semi-sweet chocolate
  chips

With an electric mixer on medium speed, beat egg until light, about one minute. Add sugar, oil and vanilla; beat well. Blend in buttermilk; set aside. Mix together flour, baking soda and salt in a large bowl. Stir in remaining ingredients; mix well. Add to egg mixture; stir until just combined. Pour batter into a greased and floured 9"x5" loaf pan. Bake at 350 degrees for one hour, or until a toothpick tests done when inserted near the center. Cool in pan for 10 minutes; remove to wire rack to cool completely. Makes one loaf.

Along with all the sweet treats, don't forget to offer icy milk, creamy cocoa or spiced cider at your bake sale. If your sale is a summer one, frosty glasses of pink lemonade will hit the spot!

Frosted Banana Bars

Karen Sampson
Waymart, PA

This is a great recipe not only for church bake sales, but it's also great for our social time after church when we get to enjoy refreshments and fellowship. Best of all, they are quick, easy, moist and delicious!

1/2 c. butter, softened
2 c. sugar
3 eggs, beaten
1-1/2 c. bananas, mashed
1/4 c. applesauce

1 t. vanilla extract
2 c. all-purpose flour
1 t. baking soda
1/2 t. salt
Optional: chopped nuts

Beat together butter and sugar in a large bowl. Beat in eggs, bananas, applesauce and vanilla; set aside. In a separate bowl, combine flour, baking soda and salt; add to butter mixture, mixing well. Spread in a greased 15"x10" jelly-roll pan. Bake at 350 degrees for 25 minutes, or until bars test done. Cool completely; spread with frosting. Garnish with nuts, if desired. Makes 3 dozen.

Frosting:

1/2 c. butter, softened
8-oz. pkg. cream cheese,
    softened

16-oz. pkg. powdered sugar
2 t. vanilla extract

Beat butter and cream cheese together. Gradually add powdered sugar and vanilla; beat well.

Top Frosted Banana Bars with a scoop of ice cream, whipped topping and a cherry...a new twist on a banana split!

Caramel Apple Tarts

Lynsey Jackson
Maryville, TN

My husband is a youth pastor so we are at the church when the doors open and our congregation LOVES to eat. I am asked to bring these sweet treats to every gathering. They're always gone before everyone can get through the buffet line, so you'd better make 2 or 3 batches!

3 Braeburn or Fuji apples,
    peeled, cored and chopped
1-1/2 c. orange juice
3 to 4 T. caramel ice cream
    topping

1 t. cinnamon
17.3-oz. pkg. frozen puff pastry
    sheets, thawed
Garnish: additional caramel ice
    cream topping, cinnamon

Combine apples, orange juice, caramel and cinnamon in a medium saucepan over medium heat. Cook until apples are tender; set aside. Cut each pastry sheet into 9 squares. Press squares into lightly greased mini muffin cups; spoon apples into cups. Bake at 350 degrees for 15 to 20 minutes. Garnish with additional caramel topping and cinnamon. Makes 1-1/2 dozen.

To get the tastiest result, reduce your oven temperature by 25 degrees if you're using glass or dark baking pans...they retain heat more than shiny pans do.

Cathy's Ice Cream Pie

Cathy Hagenow
Rockford, MI

You can use your favorite flavor of ice cream in this sweet treat.

1/3 c. corn syrup
1/3 c. peanut butter
2 c. crispy rice cereal

1/2 gal. vanilla ice cream,
    softened

Mix first 3 ingredients together; press into a greased 13"x9" baking pan. Freeze until firm. Spread softened ice cream over top; freeze again. Serves 12 to 16.

A pie-eating contest is a fun way to spend a sunny afternoon. Line up mini pies along a table, have everyone keep their hands behind their backs, then let 'em dig in!

Frosty Butter Pecan Crunch Pie

Lisa Johnson
Hallsville, TX

Chocolate and toffee come together in this scrumptious frozen pie.

2 c. graham cracker crumbs
1/2 c. butter, melted
2 3.4-oz. pkgs. instant vanilla
   pudding mix
2 c. milk
1 qt. butter pecan ice cream,
   slightly softened

8-oz. container frozen whipped
   topping, thawed
2 1.4-oz. chocolate-covered
   toffee candy bars, crushed

Combine graham cracker crumbs and melted butter in a medium bowl; pat into an ungreased 13"x9" baking pan. Freeze until firm. In a large bowl, with an electric mixer on medium speed, beat together pudding mix and milk until well blended, about one minute. Fold in ice cream and whipped topping; spoon over chilled crust. Sprinkle with candy bar pieces; freeze. Remove from freezer 20 minutes before serving. Serves 12 to 15.

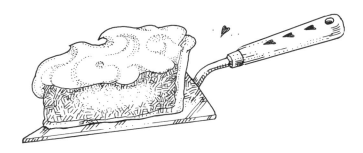

Use an alphabet cookie cutter to cut fun shapes out of fruit leather...what a fun topper for a slice of pie or a cupcake!

Cheese Danish Rolls

Diane Vasil
Plano, TX

We made this cheese roll as a fundraiser at our church. It was a wonderfully fun time for women to gather in the kitchens for the day, cooking, talking and watching the children play together.

4 c. all-purpose flour
1 c. shortening
1 c. milk, warmed
1 env. active dry yeast

3 eggs, beaten
5 T. sugar
1/4 c. butter, melted and
    divided

Combine flour and shortening in a large bowl; mix until crumbly. Heat milk to 120 to 130 degrees. Stir together remaining ingredients; add to flour mixture. Stir for 4 to 5 minutes until dough no longer sticks to the bowl. Chill for 3 to 4 hours, or overnight. Divide dough into 4 equal parts; roll each out on a floured surface into 11"x7" rectangles. Spoon filling down the center of each; roll up jelly-roll style, starting at short end. Fold edges over; seal. Arrange on 2 greased baking sheets; brush with 2 tablespoons melted butter. Bake at 375 degrees for 15 to 20 minutes, until golden. Remove from oven; brush with remaining melted butter. Cool and slice. Makes 4 rolls, each serving 10 to 12.

Filling:

4 8-oz. pkgs. cream cheese,
    softened
3 eggs, beaten

1-1/2 c. sugar
2 t. vanilla extract

Beat together all ingredients until thick and pudding-like.

Fill vintage soda bottles to the top with jimmies, sprinkles, and candy pieces...a whimsical way to serve ice cream toppers!

Sour Cream Chocolate Chip Cake

Mary Ellen Peto
Phoenixville, PA

My grandmother passed along this recipe...I can remember that at every church supper or family get-together people would be asking if she had made "her" cake. It's great for toting to church suppers or picnics because it doesn't need frosting.

6 T. butter, melted
1 c. sugar
2 eggs
1-1/3 c. all-purpose flour
1 t. baking soda

1-1/2 t. baking powder
1 t. cinnamon
8-oz. container sour cream
6-oz. pkg. semi-sweet
    chocolate chips

Blend together butter and sugar in a medium bowl; add eggs, one at a time, mixing well after each addition and set aside. Combine flour, baking soda, baking powder and cinnamon in a separate bowl. Add to butter mixture alternately with sour cream; mix well. Pour into a greased and floured 13"x9" baking pan. Sprinkle with chocolate chips. Bake at 350 degrees for 20 to 25 minutes, until golden and toothpick tests clean. Serves 12.

For bake-sale success, choose a date close to a holiday...
shoppers will be excited to buy homemade goodies
they can freeze, then simply pull out of the freezer
when the holidays are here.

2-Layer Angel Food Cake

Priscilla Robinson
Manchester, MO

My husband's grandmother was always asked to bring this cake to the ice cream social at the country church they attended for many years. Each family brought their hand-cranked ice cream maker, and spent the afternoon churning ice cream and visiting. The men would set up tables using boards and saw-horses, covered with beautiful tablecloths to set out the cakes, pies and cookies on, while the ice cream was churning.

1 env. unflavored gelatin	1 T. baking cocoa
1/4 c. cold water	1/8 t. salt
2/3 c. milk	2 c. whipping cream
2/3 c. powdered sugar	1 angel food cake, prepared

Sprinkle gelatin over water; let stand 5 minutes, until dissolved. In a small saucepan, stir together milk, sugar, cocoa and salt. Bring to a simmer over medium heat; cook for 5 minutes, stirring frequently, until smooth. Remove from heat; stir in gelatin mixture. Let stand until mixture begins to thicken. Beat cream until soft peaks form; fold carefully into cocoa mixture. Let stand until thick enough to spread on cake. With a serrated knife, slice cake horizontally into 2 layers. Spread icing between layers, around sides and over top of cake. Fill center with any remaining icing. Keep chilled. Serves 12.

Be sure to have some games for big and little kids to enjoy during your ice cream social. Old-fashioned favorites like Red Rover and sack races are sure to have everyone laughing!

Perfect Pineapple-Nut Bread

Wendy Lee Paffenroth
Pine Island, NY

Sweet with a nutty flavor.

2 c. all-purpose flour
1/2 c. sugar
1 t. baking powder
1/2 t. salt
1 c. raisins
1/2 c. chopped walnuts
1 egg, beaten

1 t. almond extract
1 t. vanilla extract
2 T. butter, melted and cooled
1 t. lemon zest
1 t. baking soda
1 c. crushed pineapple

Combine flour, sugar, baking powder and salt in a medium bowl. Add raisins and walnuts; set aside. Mix together egg, extracts, butter and lemon zest in a large bowl. Stir in flour mixture; set aside. Stir baking soda into pineapple until well blended; add to flour mixture. Pour into a greased 8"x4" loaf pan. Bake at 350 degrees for one hour. Cool on a wire rack. Makes one loaf.

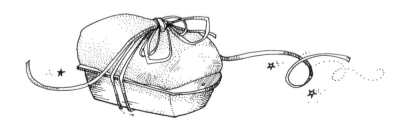

Don't forget to bring along some sugar-free varieties
of ice cream to your next social.

Angel Ice Cream Cake

Kathleen Strunk
Mesa, AZ

This recipe is very special to me and was served at a baby shower for my first daughter, Noelle. Due to a difficult pregnancy her chances for survival were very slim. Thankfully, she did survive and 23 years later is a healthy, beautiful young woman. Each time I make this dessert I am reminded that miracles do happen!

1 pt. whipping cream
3 T. sugar
1 t. vanilla extract
1 c. chopped pecans
18 coconut macaroons,
   crumbled

1/2 gal. rainbow sherbet,
   softened
1/2 gal. raspberry sherbet,
   softened
1/2 gal. vanilla ice cream,
   softened

Whip cream with sugar and vanilla until stiff peaks form; fold in pecans and cookie crumbs. Spoon half of mixture into a greased tube cake pan; layer rainbow and raspberry sherbet over top. Add a layer of vanilla ice cream; top with remaining whipped cream mixture. Cover; freeze overnight. Let stand 5 to 10 minutes before serving; insert a knife around the edge of the pan to loosen. Cut into one-inch slices. Makes 12 servings.

Whip up some soda shoppe treats at your get-together...enjoy a pink or brown cow! Add a big scoop of vanilla ice cream to a tall glass, then top off with red pop or root beer.

Chocolate Icebox Cake

Brenda Flowers
Olney, IL

This is best made the day before.

2 4-oz. pkgs. sweet baking
  chocolate, chopped
1/2 c. butter
3 T. hot water

2 T. powdered sugar
4 eggs, separated
1/2 t. vanilla extract
12 to 18 ladyfingers

Melt chocolate in a double boiler along with butter and water, stirring constantly. Stir in sugar; let mixture cool. Add egg yolks one at a time. Beat egg whites until stiff peaks form; fold into chocolate mixture. Stir in vanilla; set aside. Line bottom and sides of a lightly greased 8"x8" baking pan with a layer of ladyfingers; pour some of the chocolate mixture over the top. Cover with another layer of ladyfingers; pour remaining chocolate over top. Place in a freezer for at least 12 hours. Serves 6 to 8.

The individual cups in a muffin tin make it perfect for holding a variety of ice cream toppings…just spoon a different-flavor sprinkle or mini candy into each muffin cup.

Caramel Fudge Brownies

Sue Roberson
Peoria, AZ

This recipe came from my very special mother-in-law, and although she's no longer with us, her recipe continues to be a family favorite.

18-1/2 oz. pkg. German
   chocolate cake mix
3/4 c. butter, melted
5-oz. can evaporated milk,
   divided

1 c. semi-sweet
   chocolate chips
14-oz. pkg. caramels,
   unwrapped

Combine cake mix, butter and 1/3 cup evaporated milk. Spread half of mixture into a greased 13"x9" baking pan (this layer will be very thin). Bake at 350 degrees for 12 minutes. Melt caramels and remaining evaporated milk in a microwave-safe bowl for 3 minutes on high setting; stir and set aside. Immediately after removing from oven, sprinkle brownies with chocolate chips; pour caramel mixture over top. Spoon remaining cake batter by heaping tablespoonfuls over chocolate chips; do not mix. Bake at 350 degrees for 15 to 17 minutes. Makes 2 dozen.

When wrapping up bake sale goodies, be sure
to tuck a "Thank you" note inside.

Ms. Mabel's Butterscotch Squares

Connie Wright
Madison, TN

Over 20 years ago, I used to go to meetings at a historic church in Nashville. This is where I met Ms. Mabel, who I think was one of the best cooks I've ever met. She had little tricks for adding a special touch to everything she made...her way of sending love to each person who graced her table. This recipe is one my 29-year-old daughter continues to request for Sunday dinners.

1/2 c. butter, melted
1 c. self-rising flour
3.4-oz. pkg. instant butterscotch
   pudding mix
8-oz. pkg. cream cheese,
   softened

1 c. powdered sugar
16-oz. container frozen
   whipped topping, thawed
   and divided

Combine melted butter and flour in a small bowl. With lightly floured fingertips, pat into a lightly greased 13"x9" baking pan. Bake at 350 degrees for 20 minutes, until golden; cool completely. Prepare pudding according to package directions; refrigerate until set, about 10 minutes. With an electric mixer on low speed, beat together cream cheese, powdered sugar and one cup whipped topping until smooth. Spread over cooled crust. Spread pudding mixture over cream cheese mixture; top with remaining topping. Cover with aluminum foil; refrigerate overnight. Serves 12 to 16.

Keep bake sale pricing
simple...increments of
25 cents are good,
and it means making
change is easier for you!

assorted
PASTRIES
10¢ ea.

Caramel Sauce

Irene Robinson
Cincinnati, OH

This is delicious over ice cream, pound cake or warm pie.

1 c. brown sugar, packed   1/4 c. whipping cream
1/4 c. butter

Combine all ingredients in a small saucepan over medium heat. Bring to a boil, stirring constantly. Boil for one minute. Remove from heat; cool. Chill for one hour. Makes about one cup.

Peanut Butter Ice Cream Topping

Brenda Sinning
Lennox, SD

Spoon some of this sauce into a blender of vanilla ice cream to make yummy peanut butter milkshakes!

1 c. sugar   1/2 c. creamy peanut butter
1/2 c. water

Combine sugar and water in a small saucepan; heat until mixture boils. Boil and stir for one minute, making sure that sugar dissolves. Remove from heat; stir in peanut butter. Pour mixture into a blender; whip until creamy. Let cool; refrigerate. Makes about 1-1/2 cups.

A church social is a super time to have a Swap & Shop. Everyone brings along gently-used items they no longer need...then they can have fun swapping for items they want to take home!

Ice Cream Socials & Bake Sales

Soda Shoppe Chocolate Malts

Jill Burton
Gooseberry Patch

Good, old-fashioned fun!

8 scoops vanilla ice cream
3 c. milk
4 to 6 T. chocolate syrup

2 t. vanilla extract
1/4 c. malted milk powder

Combine all ingredients in a blender. Process until smooth and well blended. Serve immediately. Serves 4.

Skyscraper Banana Splits

Beth Kramer
Port Saint Lucie, FL

Big and little kids will line up for these!

4 T. chocolate syrup
4 scoops vanilla ice cream
4 bananas, halved lengthwise
   and crosswise

4 scoops chocolate ice cream
8 T. strawberry syrup
Garnish: whipped cream,
   maraschino cherries

Pour chocolate syrup into 4 parfait glasses; add vanilla ice cream to each. Arrange banana pieces, cut-side out, into glasses; top with chocolate ice cream. Drizzle with strawberry syrup; top with whipped cream and cherries. Makes 4 servings.

Excess on occasion is exhilarating.
    —William Somerset Maugham

Root Beer Floats

Virginia Watson
Scranton, PA

*Make sure your root beer is icy cold so the
ice cream doesn't melt too fast!*

16-oz. bottle root beer, chilled   4 scoops vanilla ice cream
   and divided

Pour 1/2 cup root beer into each of 4 tall glasses. Add a scoop of
ice cream. Carefully pour in root beer to fill glasses to top. Serves 4.

Homemade Root Beer Ice Cream

Alissa Post
New York, NY

*My family has been making this for years...
such a fun summer treat!*

4 pasteurized eggs   1 c. milk
2-1/4 c. sugar   4-1/2 t. root beer concentrate
2 qts. half-and-half   1/2 t. salt

With an electric mixer on medium speed, beat eggs until well blended.
Gradually add sugar, beating until very smooth. Add remaining
ingredients; mix well. Place in ice cream maker and freeze according
to manufacturer's instructions. Serves 16 to 20.

Dip the rim of ice cream serving bowls in melted chocolate,
then quickly dip again in sprinkles or jimmies...tasty and fun!

Brownie Sundaes

Audrey Lett
Newark, DE

Absolutely wonderful sundaes!

18-oz. pkg. refrigerated
   brownie dough
1 qt. vanilla ice cream
1 c. frozen whipped topping,
   thawed

1/2 c. chocolate syrup
6 T. mini semi-sweet
   chocolate chips
6 maraschino cherries

Prepare and bake brownies according to package directions. Cool for
20 minutes; slice into 12 pieces. Place 2 brownies in each of 6 sundae
dishes. Top with ice cream, whipped topping, chocolate syrup,
chocolate chips and cherries. Makes 6 servings.

Dress up brownies in a snap...drizzle with melted semi-sweet
chocolate, then drizzle again with melted white chocolate.

Brown Cow Milkshakes

Diana Chaney
Olathe, KS

This old-fashioned treat will be an instant hit!

3 c. chocolate ice cream
1-1/2 c. milk

1/2 c. chocolate syrup

Combine all ingredients in a blender; blend for one minute, until smooth. Serve immediately. Serves 6.

Strawberry Ice Cream Sodas

Carrie O'Shea
Marina Del Rey, CA

Be sure to use the long straws for these creamy sodas.

1 c. frozen strawberries in
  syrup, thawed
3 c. strawberry ice cream,
  divided

3 c. cream soda, chilled and
  divided
Garnish: whipped topping,
  halved strawberries

Mash thawed strawberries until well blended with syrup. Stir together strawberry syrup and one cup ice cream; divide into 4 tall glasses. Fill each glass with 2 tablespoons cream soda; scoop remaining ice cream equally into each glass. Add enough soda to fill glasses. Garnish with whipped topping and strawberries. Serves 4.

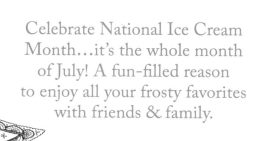

Celebrate National Ice Cream Month...it's the whole month of July! A fun-filled reason to enjoy all your frosty favorites with friends & family.

Strawberry Shortcakes

Vickie
Gooseberry Patch

For a special treat, dust each serving with a little baking cocoa.

2 pts. strawberries, hulled
   and sliced
2/3 c. plus 1/4 c. sugar, divided
2-1/3 c. biscuit baking mix

3 T. butter, melted
1/2 c. milk
3/4 c. whipping cream, whipped

Sprinkle strawberries with 2/3 cup sugar; let stand for one hour.
Combine baking mix, 3 tablespoons sugar, butter and milk until a soft
dough forms. Drop by tablespoonfuls into 6 mounds on an ungreased
baking sheet; sprinkle with remaining sugar. Bake at 425 degrees for
10 to 12 minutes. Beat whipping cream in a chilled bowl until stiff.
Split shortcakes in half; spoon strawberries between halves and tops.
Top with whipped cream. Serves 6.

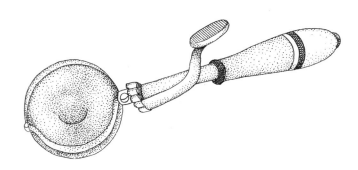

Spoon ice cream into hollowed-out lemons or oranges...
they make the prettiest little serving "bowls"!

INDEX

INDEX

INDEX

Since 1992, we've been publishing country cookbooks for every kitchen and for every meal of the day! Each has hundreds of budget-friendly recipes, using ingredients you already have on hand. Their lay-flat binding makes them easy to use and each is filled with hand-drawn artwork and plenty of personality.

Send us your favorite recipe!

and the memory that makes it special for you!* If we select your recipe for a brand-new **Gooseberry Patch** cookbook, your name will appear right along with it...and you'll receive a FREE copy of the book.

Share your recipe on our website at
www.gooseberrypatch.com
Or mail to:
Gooseberry Patch • Attn: Cookbook Dept.
PO Box 812 • Columbus, OH 43216-0812

*Don't forget to include your name, address, phone number and email address so we'll know how to reach you for your FREE book!

Find Gooseberry Patch
wherever you are!

www.gooseberrypatch.com

Call us toll-free at 1·800·854·6673

soup suppers   cake walks

spaghetti suppers

Sunday school

potlucks

ice cream socials

picnics

pancake breakfasts   bake sales

U.S. to Metric Recipe Equivalents

Volume Measurements

1/4 teaspoon	1 mL
1/2 teaspoon	2 mL
1 teaspoon	5 mL
1 tablespoon = 3 teaspoons	15 mL
2 tablespoons = 1 fluid ounce	30 mL
1/4 cup	60 mL
1/3 cup	75 mL
1/2 cup = 4 fluid ounces	125 mL
1 cup = 8 fluid ounces	250 mL
2 cups = 1 pint =16 fluid ounces	500 mL
4 cups = 1 quart	1 L

Weights

1 ounce	30 g
4 ounces	120 g
8 ounces	225 g
16 ounces = 1 pound	450 g

Oven Temperatures

300° F	150° C
325° F	160° C
350° F	180° C
375° F	190° C
400° F	200° C
450° F	230° C

Baking Pan Sizes

Square	
8x8x2 inches	2 L = 20x20x5 cm
9x9x2 inches	2.5 L = 23x23x5 cm

Rectangular	
13x9x2 inches	3.5 L = 33x23x5 cm

Loaf	
9x5x3 inches	2 L = 23x13x7 cm

Round	
8x1-1/2 inches	1.2 L = 20x4 cm
9x1-1/2 inches	1.5 L = 23x4 cm